The Complete Sausage Cookbook

The Complete Sausage Cookbook

by **Pamela Riddle** and
Mary Jane Danley

Illustrations by Judith Nissenbaum

SAN FRANCISCO BOOK COMPANY, INC.

San Francisco 1977

Printed in the United States of America

Library of Congress Cataloging in Publication Data

Riddle, Pamela, 1946-
    The complete sausage cookbook.

    Includes index.
    1. Sausages.   2.   Cookery (Sausages)   I.   Danley,
Mary Jane, 1947-   joint author.   II.   Title.
TX749.R62   641.6′6   77-70226
ISBN 0-913374-62-8
ISBN 0-913374-63-6 pbk.

For our mother, AGNES RIDDLE, *one of the world's great cooks.*

With special thanks to PAUL SCHULMAN *and* JOHN DANLEY
for the hours of typing, tasting, babysitting, and emotional support so freely given.

Contents

Introduction

The kitchen is the traditional heart of the home. This was true of the homes we grew up in, and it is true of the homes we have since made for ourselves. Our earliest years were spent in an area of Manhattan known as Yorkville. Now it's the Upper East Side, where swinging singles living in luxury towers have replaced the Czechoslovakian families in their six-story walk-ups. Then, all of the small businesses were owned by Czechs and transactions were conducted bilingually. The delicious smell of roasting coffee beans wafted out of Sazama's and you couldn't walk past Hajek's Bakery without craving something sweet and buttery. A hearty and thoroughly fattening meal could be enjoyed at the Praha Restaurant and then worked off at the Sokol Hall gym.

We and our parents shared two first-floor apartments with our maternal grandmother—known to all as Babi—and bachelor Uncle Joe. These were, in fact, the same rooms in which our mother and all seven of her brothers and sisters had been raised. The building was one of seven planted around an interior courtyard. Aunts, uncles, and cousins lived all around us in adjoining buildings, but Babi's was "home" to everyone. Three generations of our family dreamed, did homework, learned to speak English, read, write, and tell time, gossiped, argued and made up again around Babi's huge kitchen table.

Coffee was brewing continuously at Babi's and homemade jams, jellies, breads, cakes, pies, and cookies were all part of our daily fare. The wonderful meals were homemade too, right down to the noodles in the soup. Babi had been trained as a cook in Vienna and passed her skills on to her daughters, daughters-in-law, and granddaughters. Her legacy is all the more precious because she taught us that good cooking goes beyond the preparation of tasty foods, becoming an act of love.

Every Sunday Babi rolled out pastry and our mother prepared fruits and spices for the strudels, pies, and cakes they baked for the regular family gatherings. Even as preschoolers we worked alongside them, busily preparing cookie dough, learning to roll, pinch, and test it before ever-so-carefully cutting out circles with the open ends of juice glasses. Our contributions were baked along with theirs. Later, they were displayed prominently on the groaning sideboard, while we stood, beaming, to receive the astonished accolades. This ritual survived the passage of time and a move to the suburbs. Our cooking did, however, become more sophisticated. By adolescence we were turning out such concoctions as beef Wellington and croquembouche with chocolate sauce, faithfully transcribed and prepared according to Julia Child's televised instructions.

Now that we are both skilled cooks, the pleasure we find in preparing and sharing food has not diminished. And since the quality of commercial foods has gone down while the prices have risen, doing it ourselves is an economic, nutritious, and creative alternative, a way to avoid the harmful chemicals, insects, rodent parts, and other execrable stuff in processed foods. A small investment in a home vegetable garden has enabled us to feed our whole families the year round. Baking our own breads, preserving, pickling, and drying has saved us money and allowed us to control quality and taste. We've even tried a bit of home smoking with farm-fresh hams and bacon and fresh-caught fish. The results are wonderful.

With our Czech heritage, a good kielbasa has always been every morsel as good as any apple pie—except, of course, Babi's. And although we did not learn sausagemaking at her knee, it was natural that we should come to discover it. Experiments in home smoking led us to try sausages. Our first attempt was Italian hot sausages. One taste convinced us that mushy, mealy, store-bought sausages would never pass our lips again. After griddle cakes with our own breakfast sausage, and barbecued liulia, there was no stopping us. We were hooked, and we began to collect all of the recipes for making and serving sausages that we share here.

8   Commercial sausages are full of fat, fillers, and chemicals, but homemade sausages are firm and meaty with a good, solid texture. Some butchers make their own sausages, but although the taste and quality are both excellent, the price is high. With homemade sau-

sages, economy is maintained—we have yet to make any that cost more per pound than a "good" commercial variety.

We have also discovered that sausagemaking is fun. Since there are enough things to do to keep several people busy, your family or friends can participate. There's trimming and grinding the meat, preparing and stuffing the casings, tying off (an excellent job for children), and even smoking the finished product (this is a lot easier than you think—we'll tell you how to manage it with just a home barbecue).

And, sausagemaking is creative cooking. Because there are no hard and fast rules, a little more of this or a little less of that doesn't spell disaster, as it would with a soufflé. The process inspires invention. You start out following a recipe, and before you know it you are following your own tastes.

We've found that sausages exist in nearly all national cuisines and there are enough different kinds to please everybody, from peasant-style aromatic blends to delicately spiced and prepared varieties. And, the equipment couldn't be any cheaper or easier to find—you can make do with just a wooden spoon and a funnel.

The scope of information we present here is not found anywhere else. Many of the recipes come from our friends and their mothers and grandmothers, and have never been printed. We have included a glossary that describes over 100 of the different kinds of sausages you might come across in this country. We are sharing what we have learned and collected in the hope that others will try sausagemaking and enjoy this often-neglected art as much as we do.

Experiment, enjoy, and share—satisfaction is sure to follow!

PAMELA RIDDLE   9
MARY JANE DANLEY

New York
February 1977

About Sausage

Sausages have been around practically since people began to cook. One of the earliest references we've come across dates from about 800 B.C. The Greek poet Homer wrote in the *Odyssey:*

". . . a man near a great glowing fire turns to and fro a sausage full of fat and blood, anxious to have it quickly roast; so to and fro Odysseus tossed and pondered."

The salami that we love to eat today originated in the ancient Cypriot city of Salamis. That city was destroyed in 449 B.C., making salami well over 2500 years old.

The ancient Roman poet Petronius wrote in his *Satyricon:* "There were sausages too, smoking hot on a silver grill." In 1853 historian A. Soyer wrote about Greek civilization in *The Pantropheon,* and referred to a banquet which took place in A.D. 64. Included on the menu were egg and mushroom sausages, pheasant sausages, and lobster sausages.

Sausages were also being eaten in other parts of the world. A menu survives of a banquet given in the court of King Srenika in India, circa A.D. 1000. Mandaliya, a spicy marrow sausage broiled over charcoals, was served.

By the beginning of the Middle Ages sausages were common throughout Europe. People of the area that is now Germany, Poland, and Austria were making the same hearty wursts, served with soups and cabbage, that we love today.

During the Crusades of the 1500s, it is said, the enemy armies besieging the city of Troyes in France fell to eating the local specialty, andouilles, with such gusto and became so preoccupied with eating them that the people of Troyes had time to regroup and drive them back.

The process of sausagemaking evolved in every country as an effort to economize and make use of whatever scraps of meat were left over after an animal had been butchered. The procedure of stuffing meat into casings remains basically the same today, but sausage recipes have been greatly refined and good sausagemaking is a highly respected culinary art.

11

Unscrupulous commercial sausagemakers are no doubt responsible for the mistaken notion that many people have about sausages—that they are made from impure parts of animals. In truth, good sausage chefs are as discriminating about choosing what goes into their products as a winemaker is about selecting grapes. However, the criteria used for choosing meat for the table are not necessarily valid when choosing meat for sausages. Just as it would be ridiculous to waste filet mignon on a stew, it should not be used for sausages either. Animal hair, chemicals, and fillers full of empty calories are often found in commerical sausage products; they are not only undesirable, but can be harmful as well. The tougher, bonier cuts of meat used in homemade sausages are not. Unsuitable for the table, these cuts become delightful to eat and easy to digest once they are ground. The same holds true for most of the organ meats, and even the blood. As undesirable as they may seem in their natural states, they can be delicious when ground, spiced, and cased. These less "perfect" parts of the animal are as high in protein and nutrition as the rest. The beauty is that in using them to make sausages there is no waste and high nutritional standards are maintained.

It would be impossible to estimate the number of different kinds of sausages that exist today. Every culture has its own varieties, every variety has seven or eight or more variations, and every sausage chef has a favorite recipe for each one. We asked many cooking experts and sausage *aficionados* to guess how many different kinds there are, and received replies of from several hundred to several thousand. What we do know for sure is that every nation has its own specialties. The German varieties are the best known, but we've also collected delicious recipes from such faraway places as the Dominican Republic and China.

There are six basic kinds of sausages:

SMOKED SAUSAGES are made from meats that have been cured and then smoked over wood fires. Smoked sausages can be either cooked (hot dogs, bologna) or uncooked (mettwurst).

COOKED SAUSAGES (liverwurst, boudin noir), are made from meats that are either fresh or preserved by curing.

FRESH SAUSAGES are made from ground meats that have not been cooked or cured (breakfast sausage, bratwurst).

DRY SAUSAGES are made from fresh meats that have been spiced (chorizo, dry salami), cured for several days, then dried for varying, but long, periods of time.

NEW-CONDITIONED SAUSAGES (cervelat) are made of meats with spices and curing ingredients mixed in. Then they are cured for a few days and smoked.

SPECIALTY SAUSAGES can be prepared in any of the ways listed. They are made from unusual combinations of meats or grains, vegetables, and spices that are blended together and cased.

In order to familiarize you with the different kinds of sausages, we've prepared a glossary of over 100 of the most well-known varieties. Browsing through it will be informative, and it will be a handy reference. In each case, the country of origin is noted and a brief description and ingredients given. Sausages in bold type will reappear in the recipe section.

ALESSANDRI SALAMI. *American.* Beef and pork seasoned with salt, black pepper, sugar, and whole peppercorns, and dried for six months.

ANDOUILLES, ANDOUILLETTES. *French.* These are pork chitterlings or tripe sausages seasoned with pepper, salt, nutmeg, ginger, and cinammon. Sometimes bay leaf, onions, and mushrooms or parsley are added. Andouillettes are simply small andouilles.

APPENNINO SAUSAGE. *Italian.* A dry salamilike type made of pork and beef seasoned with garlic, sugar, mustard, salt, and pepper, then air-dried.

AUGSBURGERWURST. *German.* Lean pork and bacon fat seasoned with salt, pepper, cloves, and nutmeg and cased in beef gut. First the sausage is dried, then lightly smoked.

BAUERNWURST. *German.* Coarsely ground pork seasoned with salt, pepper, garlic, and whole mustard seeds, then smoked.

BAYERISCHE BOCKWURST. *German.* Bavarian-style bockwurst consisting of veal and pork mixed with cream, chives, onion, mace, and nutmeg, and stuffed into sheep rather than hog casings.

BERLINER BOCKWURST. *German.* Beef and pork seasoned with garlic, paprika, salt, and sugar, then smoked. Similar to the American hot dog.

BIROLDO TOSCANO. *Italian.* A pork blood sausage, lightly seasoned, with raisins added.

BLUTWURST. *German.* Made with beef blood, pork fat, and finely ground pork, bound with gelatin (rather than the usual egg and bread crumbs) and packed into very large casings.

BOCKWURST. *German.* Originally a spring sausage, but now available all year. It is made from veal, pork, milk, eggs, onions, parsley, chives, and leeks.

BOLOGNA. *Italian* (really!). A mixture of beef and pork, often seasoned with sage, cayenne, paprika, salt, and black pepper. One kind is put in natural casing, another is cased in muslin, and a third is simply wrapped with string.

14

BOTERHAMWORST. *Dutch.* A veal and pork mixture that is first cured, then seasoned with ginger, nutmeg, mace, and pepper, and finally smoked.

BOUDIN BLANC. *French.* Translates as "white pudding." There are dozens of regional varieties, but it is usually made of pork or chicken combined with bread crumbs, cream, and light seasoning. Occasionally truffles are added. It may be cased or not.

BOUDIN NOIR. *French.* This time "black pudding." Actually a kind of blood sausage usually made of pork, blood, suet, eggs, cream, onions, brandy, and spices. Often vegetables are added, such as spinach or endive, as well as nuts, raisins, and even semolina. It may be cased or uncased.

BOUDIN DE LAPIN. *French.* Made with rabbit or hare and pork tenderloin ground very finely and seasoned with parsley, tarragon, chives, salt, nutmeg, ginger, cinnamon, and, occasionally, cloves. Sometimes the liver of the rabbit is chopped finely and added. This may be cased or uncased and is highly perishable.

BOUDIN DU LANGUEDOC. *French.* Pork and blood flavored with onions and caraway or anise. It may be cased or not.

BRATWURST. *German.* Veal and pork seasoned with ginger, mustard, and coriander. Regional varieties are also seasoned with mace, nutmeg, or sage.

BUTIFARA CATALANE. *Spanish.* Pork head cheese flavored with oregano. This is very hard to come by.

CALABRESE SALAMI. *Italian.* Pork seasoned heavily with hot pepper and garlic, then air-dried.

CAMBRIDGE PORK SAUSAGE. *English.* Equal portions of lean and fat pork seasoned with mustard, allspice, mace, cayenne, ginger, salt, and pepper. Rice and rusk are added as fillers.

CAPICOLLA. *Italian.* Boneless pork shoulder spiced with red pepper and cased—not ground, but pressed.

CERVELAT. *French.* Lean pork spiced with parsley, thyme, basil, nutmeg, and cloves, and sometimes scallions or pimiento. The sausages are tied into eight-inch lengths and dried.

CERVELATWURST. *German.* Pork and beef in equal proportions, finely chopped and seasoned with salt, mustard, and black and red pepper.

ČEVAPČIĆI. *Yugoslavian.* Beef and veal spiced with garlic, parsley, and paprika. Made without casings.

CHIPOLATA. *Spanish.* A small sausagelike chorizo, with the texture of a frankfurter.

CHORIZO. *Spanish.* Beef and pork seasoned with hot pepper, garlic, salt, pepper, chili, sugar, vinegar, and sometimes pimiento. There are many regional varieties. Can be found fresh, but is usually smoked and dried.

CHUB BOLOGNA. *American.* Beef and pork ground with bacon to a smooth texture and lightly seasoned.

CIPOLLATA. *Italian.* Pork combined with rice and rusk, then seasoned with coriander, nutmeg, thyme, salt, and pepper.

COSENZA. *Italian.* Beef and pork spiced with garlic, red pepper, coriander, whole peppercorns, and sugar—characterized by its fat, stubby shape. Usually smoked.

COTECHINO. *Italian.* Fresh pork sausage flavored with garlic, coriander, and hot pepper. Some are stuffed into pigs' feet—which doesn't sound easy.

16   COTTO SALAMI. *Italian.* A soft, cooked salami of cured beef and pork seasoned with garlic, salt, pepper, sugar, and whole peppercorns.

CRÉPINETTES. *French.* Small, flat pork sausages wrapped in caul fat rather than put in casings. There are regional variations in seasonings, which may include brandy or wine, pepper, salt, thyme, sage, parsley, cinnamon, or cumin. Pistachio nuts, chestnuts, and truffles are common additions.

CROQUANTS. *French.* Pork and beef heavily spiced with cumin, red and black pepper, and garlic.

CUCKOLDS. *English.* Venison sausage spiced with onion. Oatmeal is added and the mixture is stuffed into venison tripe skins.

ENGLISH BLACK PUDDING. *English.* An extremely heavy and thick blood pudding that is definitely an acquired taste. Made of beef blood, barley, oatmeal, and flour flavored with onions, salt, pepper, coriander, celery seeds, mustard, and allspice.

ENGLISH FAGGOTS. *English.* Pork shoulder combined with pork liver and kidney and seasoned with onions, garlic, sage, salt, pepper, and mace. The mixture is bound with beaten egg and bread crumbs, and cased in caul fat.

ESCAROLA IMBOTTITA. *Italian.* Italian pork sausage seasoned with garlic, parsley, olives, pine nuts, basil, oregano, and capers. Bread crumbs are added and the mixture is cased in cooked escarole.

FLEISCHWURST. *German.* All beef, or pork and beef, flavored with garlic, paprika, salt, and pepper, and lightly smoked. Similar to bologna in taste.

FRENCH GARLIC SAUSAGE. *French.* A garlic sausage made of pork, heavy doses of garlic, and smaller amounts of cayenne, ginger, cinnamon, nutmeg, pepper, and brandy. It is dried for as long as five months before eating.

FRENCH LIVER SAUSAGE. *French.* Pork liver and salt pork chopped and seasoned with nutmeg, cloves, cinnamon, kirsch, salt, pepper, and sometimes onions, then dried.

FRIZZES, FRIZZIES. *Italian.* A dry, salamilike sausage made of beef and pork flavored with anise and hot pepper. There's also a "sweet" variety, which is spicy, but not gum-rending like the hot one.

GALICIAN SAUSAGE. *Spanish.* Cured beef and pork seasoned with garlic and coriander, cooked, then heavily smoked and air-dried.

GÄNSEBRUST. *German.* Goose meat that has been smoked, ground, and wrapped in goose skin.

GEHIRNWURST. *German.* Made from pork brains cooked in brine and seasoned with mace, salt, and pepper.

GERAUCHERTE BRATWURST. *German.* Very lean pork and bacon mixed with salt and pepper, heavily smoked, and dried.

GOGUE. *French.* A black and white pudding made for the Christmas and Easter holidays. Pig's blood mixed with cream and milk and seasoned with egg, onion, bread crumbs, salt, pepper, and beet leaves. The sausage is stuffed into large casings, poached, and dried.

GÖTEBORG. *Swedish.* Pork and beef seasoned with thyme, cardamom, salt, pepper, and sugar, then heavily smoked and dried.

GOTHAER CERVELAT. *German.* All pork, very finely textured and heavily salted.

GRUETZWURST. *German.* Pork and beef extended with oatmeal and flavored with onion, sage, allspice, and summer savory.

HAGGIS. *Scottish.* Not sausage in the usual sense. A sheep's stomach is stuffed with ground sheep's liver and heart, beef suet, onion, and oatmeal. Traditionally it is then steamed and served on New Year's Eve.

18

HEAD CHEESE. *All countries.* Not a cheese, but a jellied meat mixture made from the head or shoulder of a hog, with many regional variations. It is often seasoned with onion, carrots, thyme, sage, bay leaf, lemon juice, sherry, black pepper, some veal or chicken or ham, and a bit of tongue. Gelatin is added, and the mixture is chilled. It is then sliced and served with sliced Bermuda onion, chopped egg, and vinaigrette sauce.

HOLSTEINER SAUSAGE. *German.* A soft beef cervelat, mildly seasoned, but heavily smoked.

IRISH PORK SAUSAGE. *Irish.* Lean pork and fatback, seasoned with garlic, salt, basil, thyme, rosemary, and marjoram. Highly perishable.

JAGTWURST. *German.* Coarsely ground pork and beef, lightly seasoned, with pistachio nuts added.

JITERNICE. *Czechoslovakian.* Made from pork liver combined with pork and pork snouts, finely chopped, and flavored with allspice, garlic, marjoram, salt, and pepper. Barley, or sometimes rice, is added.

KABANOS. *Polish and Ukranian.* Smoked pork and beef flavored with garlic and mace.

KIELBASA. *Polish.* Pork, beef, and veal spiced with garlic, allspice, marjoram, salt, pepper, and sometimes caraway.

KISKA. *Russian.* Made of fat trimmings, buckwheat groats, salt, pepper, onions, and blood. It tastes much better than it sounds.

KNACKWURST, KNOCKWURST, KNOBLAUCH. *All German for the same thing.* Beef and pork with a strong garlic flavor. Can be smoked.

KÖNIGSWURST. *German.* It means literally "king's sausage." Made from partridges, truffles, mushrooms, beaten eggs, wine, salt, pepper, and mace. You can substitute Cornish hens, since they are more readily available.

KRACKAUER. *Polish.* Lean pork and beef seasoned with garlic and black pepper, then cooked and smoked.

KRAKOWSKA. *Polish and Ukrainian.* Pork shoulder seasoned with salt, pepper, mace, caraway seeds, and garlic, then smoked.

LANDJAGER. *Swiss.* Beef and pork that is heavily salted, smoked, and dried.

LAONA BOLOGNA. *Italian.* Beef and pork with a very spicy garlic flavor.

LEBANON BOLOGNA. *American.* Once made only by farmers in Lebanon, Pennsylvania, but now more widely available. The recipes are jealously guarded, but usually include beef flavored with garlic, cloves, coriander, and ginger.

LIULIA. *Armenian.* Ground lamb seasoned heavily with garlic and mint. Made only without casings.

LIVERWURST. *German.* Liver sausage with a host of regional varieties. Basically pork liver mixed with pork and seasoned with salt, white pepper, allspice, and onion. Infinite variations include the addition of such things as truffles, wine, garlic, various nuts, and even anchovies.

LONGANZINA, LINGUISA. *Portuguese and Brazilian.* Lean pork seasoned with red pepper, garlic, cumin, and cinnamon, then cured in vinegar and heavily smoked.

LOUKANIKA. *Greek.* Lamb and pork flavored with orange rind, allspice, and garlic.

LYON SAUSAGE. *French.* Well-trimmed pork mixed with salt pork, salt, pepper, garlic, and white peppercorns. These are huge—up to 18 inches in length, with each holding eight

20

to ten pounds of meat. They are dried for a week, then tied with string to keep them straight, and dried for several months more.

MECKLENBURGER BRATWURST. *German.* Equal proportions of lean and fat pork are ground to a smooth texture and seasoned with salt, pepper, allspice, lemon rind, and brandy.

MEDWURST. *Swedish.* Beef and pork that is cured and flavored with coriander, then dried.

METTWURST. *German.* A form of liverwurst made with finely ground pork liver, blandly seasoned with coriander, salt, and pepper, then lightly cured and smoked. This is spreadable.

NÜRNBERGERWURST. *German.* Lean pork and bacon fat seasoned with salt, pepper, thyme, nutmeg, marjoram, and kirsch.

OXFORD PORK SAUSAGE. *English.* Pork trimmings seasoned with salt and sugar only, then cooked and smoked.

PEPPERONI CASERTA. *Italian.* This is very hot—beef and pork heavily flavored with hot pepper, garlic, sugar, salt, and pepper, then air-dried.

PEPPERONI DOLCE. *Italian.* The same as pepperoni caserta, but with garlic and hot pepper used in less dragonlike amonunts.

PINKELWURST. *German.* A lean pork and oatmeal mixture that is very bland. It is simmered with kale.

POLNISCHEWURST. *German.* Pork and pork fat seasoned with salt, pepper, pimiento, and cloves. The sausage is held together with pork blood, then cased, dried, and smoked.

POTATISKORV. *Swedish.* Beef, or beef and veal, combined with potatoes and onions and seasoned with allspice, sugar, and white and black pepper.

PRESKY. *Czechoslovakian.* Cured pork trimmings seasoned lightly with salt, pepper, garlic, and allspice, then smoked.

RILLETTES. *French.* Breast of pork simmered in lard, seasoned with salt, pepper, and poultry seasoning. It is poured, still simmering, into jars and covered with waxed paper or sealed with lard.

RINDFLEISCHWURST. *German.* Lean beef and pork fat seasoned with salt, pepper, and coriander, with saltpeter added. The sausages are tied in pairs after being cased, and dried for 48 hours before serving.

SALSICCIA SPECIALE. *Italian.* A fresh pork sausage seasoned with garlic, coriander, fennel, and various other spices. It has a short and stubby shape.

SALSIZ. *Swiss.* Beef and pork seasoned with mace, sage, cardamom, pepper, and sugar. It is lightly smoked, then cooked.

SARDELOWA. *Polish.* Pork mixed with veal and beef, lightly spiced, and stuffed into a large casing. This is thick and horseshoe shaped when finished.

SAUCISSES DE CAMPAGNE. *French.* Coarse pork and fatback flavored with red wine, ginger, cinnamon, nutmeg, and garlic. Usually juniper berries and shallots are added and the whole is stuffed into the largest casing available.

SAUCISSE DE CERVELLE. *French.* The same as German gehirnwurst. The French serve it with beans, the Germans with sauerkraut.

SAUCISSES DE MADRILÈNES. *French.* Veal, pork fat, and sardine fillets packed in oil and cased in small beef gut. The cased sausages are tied into rings.

SAUCISSE DE STRASBOURG. *French.* Brine-cured pork mixed with fatback and seasoned with mace, nutmeg, cinnamon, and coriander.

SAUCISSE DE VIENNE. *French.* Pork, veal, and beef flavored with coriander and cayenne, then lightly smoked.

SAUCISSON À TRANCHER. *French.* Ground sow's belly seasoned with garlic and parsley, cooked, and dried for at least a month.

SAUCISSON AU FOIE DE VOLAILLE. *French.* A chicken liver sausage seasoned with white pepper, savory, cinnamon, sage, nutmeg, and thyme. Cognac and cream cheese are added to enhance the texture. This is used like paté.

SAUCISSON CERVELAT ORDINAIRE. *French.* Coarsely chopped pork and fat stuffed into beef casings and tied off at eight- to ten-inch intervals, then smoked for one to five days.

SAUCISSON CUIT AU MADÈRE. *French.* A large, finely textured pork sausage seasoned with pepper, nutmeg, red wine, truffles, and pistachio nuts.

SAUCISSON D'ARLES. *French.* Beef and pork salami flavored with salt, black pepper, sugar, and whole peppercorns. Dried as long as six months.

SAUCISSON DE BOURGOGNE. *French.* Pork and fatback seasoned with ginger, cinnamon, nutmeg, pepper, and kirsch.

SAUCISSON DE PÉRIGORD. *French.* Pork and fatback with white wine, nutmeg, ginger, pepper, and truffles.

SCOTTISH SAUSAGE. *Scottish.* Fresh pork sausage seasoned with mace and sage and wrapped in caul fat.

SCHINKENWURST. *German.* A mildly seasoned sausage made with ham.

SCHWABISCHEWURST. *German.* Lean pork flavored with garlic, caraway, and pepper. Very smooth textured. It can be eaten fresh or lightly smoked.

SCRAPPLE. *American.* Technically not a sausage, but rather a loaf prepared from minced meats combined with cornmeal and a variety of seasonings, often including marjoram, cloves, thyme, and sage.

SERDELOWA, SERDELKI. *Polish.* A fairly bland pork sausage seasoned with coriander, nutmeg, and peppercorns. Serdelowa is made into large rings, serdelki into small links.

SOPPRESSATA. *Italian.* A dry salami made of beef and pork, seasoned with a lot of garlic and air-dried.

SULC, SULZE, SOUSE, **SYLTA.** *Middle European and Scandinavian.* Pork head meats and tongue mixed with the gelatin extracted in cooking them. Some types are pickled.

THURINGER. *Alpine.* Pork and veal spiced with mace, coriander, celery seed, and ginger. Milk or dry milk solids are added, and the sausage is cooked.

TOULOUSE SAUSAGE. *French.* The sausage made famous in cassoulet. Pork neck or shoulder mixed with fatback and seasoned blandly with salt, sugar, white pepper, white wine, and a touch of garlic.

WIENERWURST. *German.* The hot dog. Beef and pork mixed with flour, coriander, mace, and onion.

WEISS BRATWURST. *German.* Pork and veal mixed with milk-soaked white bread and bacon fat, then seasoned with white pepper, lemon rind, and nutmeg.

WEISSWURST. *German.* Usually made for Oktoberfest. Veal and pork seasoned with sage, thyme, and mace.

WURSTCHEN. *German.* Very small sausages (three inches) cased in sheep's gut. Made from pork and veal seasoned with salt, pepper, cardamom, and pimiento, mixed with Rhine wine. The sausages are tied into bunches.

WURSTE VON KALBSGEKRASE. *German.* Made from calf's mesentery (stomach membrane) that is first blanched, then cooked in vinegar and simmered in a court bouillon. Finally, it is chopped and mixed with salt, pepper, nutmeg, eggs, and heavy cream. The mixture is stuffed into pork casings and tied off at ten-inch intervals.

ZUNGENWURST. *German.* A blood sausage made with pork blood, pork fat, ground pork, and veal tongue. Completely cooked and smoked.

ZWEIBELWURST. *German.* Pork liver, pork, and veal flavored with browned onions. This has a smooth, even texture and is highly perishable.

Making Sausage

There are two basic ways to make sausages and both are very simple. For one method, you need the sausage-stuffing attachment on a meat grinder, but for the other, all you need is an ordinary, large, household funnel and a wooden spoon. Whichever method you use will require meat for the filling and material for the casing, so let's consider these items first.

Most sausages are made from pork, beef, or veal used alone or in various combinations. The choicest cuts of meat are not necessary for sausages, so keep this in mind when you are selecting meats for the sausages you want to make. The most economical and efficient cuts of pork to use are from the neck and shoulder. These are also suitable veal choices, as is the breast. Watch for sales and take advantage of them; your sausages will never suffer from choice cuts of pork or veal. Be very careful about trimming the meat, or have your butcher do a thorough job of it. You'll want to be certain that no traces of gristle or bone remain.

Choosing beef for sausagemaking is a slightly different matter. The cheaper, fattier cuts, such as chuck, tend to be tastier and will do more to enhance the finished product. Shin beef is another good choice. You can still watch for sales, but don't worry about capturing the more expensive cuts—just get the cheap cuts even more cheaply and save the sirloin for the table.

Occasionally, you'll find lamb or poultry called for in a recipe. Any kind of fowl will serve for the poultry. Lamb, though, is a little tricky. We do not recommend using it in combination with any other meat. The strong taste of lamb can overpower other meats and make the mixture too fatty. Lamb sausages are not usually cased and the meat is used only with appropriate spices.

With any meat you buy, always remember to allow for fat and bone. A four-pound piece of pork with bone and fat will not yield four pounds of pork meat. You may need up to five pounds to get the amount of meat you need. Nothing goes to waste, though, because you can usually make use of the fat in the sausages you'll be making, or freeze it for another time.

While we are on the subject, you will notice that most sausage recipes call for a certain amount of fat. You can minimize the amount that goes into the sausages you make, but do not try to eliminate fat completely as an ingredient. The fat serves several purposes, adding to the flavor, helping to bind the mixture of meat and seasonings, and lubricating the casing. You may have to buy the fat you'll need separately, but remember that you will be trimming some fat off of the meat you are using. Always reserve these trimmings—or retrieve them from the butcher—they may be just the amount you'll need. If you need to buy extra fat, be certain to get exactly what the recipe calls for. Salt pork and fatback, for example, should be used only in the small amounts specified. They are very salty and soaking or rinsing will not remove the strong taste. If you use too much of either, you may ruin the sausages.

When you buy the meat, you'll also be able to purchase the casings. These are the tubes into which the sausage meat is stuffed. Casings are usually the intestines of hogs, cattle, or sheep. They come in widths of from one to four inches and are packaged dry or salted. Most sausages are made with pork casings. Beef casings are used for sausages that are large and require thicker casings—bologna is one example. Natural casings such as these add to the flavor of the sausages. In addition, they help to retain the sausage shape and will stretch and shrink along with it.

Sometimes a recipe will call for muslin casing, usually for a very large smoked sausage. Like natural casing, muslin casing will seal in the flavor of the sausage. It is essentially a cloth bag, which you can make with little effort. Just fold a piece of unbleached muslin in half, and outline the general size of the sausage you wish to make. Cut out with pinking shears and stitch a half-inch seam, leaving one end open for stuffing.

You will find some salamis and pepperonis coated with paraffin. This is another method of preserving flavor; it also prevents decay. There are many casings available on the market made of plastic or other manufactured materials. We experimented with them for this book, but we found that they cost more than natural casings and add nothing to the sausages. We missed that extra dash of flavor that natural casings supply, and we found the natural casings more aesthetically pleasing.

With grinder or funnel and spoon and casings ready, you need only to assemble the spices you'll be using, a large bowl for mixing them with the meat, some string for tying off the sausages, and you'll be ready to begin.

First, prepare the casing. Remove the length of casing you will need and rinse it under running water. Soak it in a bowl of lukewarm water for about one-half hour, changing the water two or three times. When the soaking time is over, bring the casing back over to the tap and slip two fingers into one of the ends to separate the sides. Hold this end under running water for a couple of minutes, letting the water flow through the length of the casing and out the other end. If the casing you are using has an inner membrane, remove it at this point. Drain the well-rinsed casing and set aside until you're ready for stuffing. Return any unused casing to its original container and repack with salt. Stored in a refrigerator or freezer, natural casings preserved in this manner should last for about two years.

While the casing is soaking for that half hour, you can prepare the meat mixture. The meat and fat can be either run through a grinder—the method we prefer—or chopped by hand. (Of course, the butcher can do it for you, but it's much more fun to do it yourself.) If you are using a grinder, run a bit of fat through first to oil up the works, then grind meat and fat alternately. If you are chopping—and this works well if you like a meatier, somewhat coarser sausage—be sure to use a very sharp knife. Chop the meat into one-fourth-inch pieces. A friend's mother taught us to freeze or partially freeze the meat and fat, which makes them much easier to cut. Work with the fat in small quantities, since it tends to warm up more quickly than the meat.

After grinding, place the meat in a large bowl and mix thoroughly. This is most easily

29

done with your hands. Now add the spices and flavorings called for in the recipe. Blend in, still using your hands, until they are spread evenly throughout the mixture.

If you are making a large batch of sausage, doubling or tripling a recipe, mixing in a bowl may be impossible. Thoroughly clean the top of a large table or several large pastry boards. After grinding the meat, spread it out on the table in an even layer. Sprinkle the appropriate spices evenly over the meat, and mix in with your hands. The sausages may then be cased in the manner described below.

We must take a moment to add a word of caution here. DO NOT TAKE ANY TASTES OF THE MEAT MIXTURE IF THERE IS PORK IN IT!! The mixture will smell wonderful and look deceptively like ground beef. However, trichinosis, a disease you can get from eating raw pork, is no laughing matter. Poultry, too, can cause illness when eaten raw; it carries the salmonella bacteria. *Be certain to keep your hands and utensils away from your mouth at all times when you are handling pork or poultry products.* And thoroughly clean wooden spoons and boards used in preparing them, especially if you will later use these utensils to prepare foods that will be served raw.

After the meat is prepared, it's time to stuff the casings. If you are using either a manual or an electric grinder, replace the grinding attachment with the sausage-stuffing nozzle. Take one end of the prepared casing (it should still be damp) and slip two fingers into one of the openings, then slide the opening over the outside of the nozzle. Slip the rest of the casing onto the nozzle, using both fingers to keep it even and untwisted. It will begin to form accordionlike pleats as you slide it on. Don't be delicate about it—it can overlap as much as it needs to.

When the full length of the casing is on the nozzle, run some of the meat mixture through the grinder until it is flush with the very tip of the nozzle. This prevents unwanted air from being forced into the casing ahead of the meat mix. Next, pull about one and one-half inches of casing off of the nozzle and tie it tightly with a small length of string. Keeping the thumb and forefinger of one hand on the casing as a guide, begin forcing the meat mixture into the casing. You will quickly develop a feel for this. You will see how easily the mixture goes in and how to most comfortably control the length and thickness of the sausage link. When a link reaches the desired size, twist the casing a couple of times and tie it off with a small length of string, then continue stuffing and tying off until the casing is used up. After tying off a few links, you'll feel like an old hand at it.

Watch out for air bubbles and holes or breaks in the casing. Jab air bubbles with a needle. As soon as you stuff a few links, you should have them under control. If the casing should break or tear while you are stuffing it, tie off the sausage at that point and continue to stuff the undamaged portion. Keep in mind that you don't have to stuff the sausages to the breaking point, although you may tend to do so at first. Stop stuffing when each link is just a little less thick than you want it to be. The meat mixture contained within will expand as you cook the sausages and you don't want them to burst while cooking.

31

If you are using a funnel and spoon, slide the casing onto the spout of the funnel, as described for the nozzle on the meat grinder. If you are right-handed, hold the funnel in your left arm; if you are left-handed, hold it in your right arm. Crook the arm and hold the funnel up close to your body. Pack the bowl of the funnel with the meat mixture and force it down into the spout with a wooden spoon until the meat is flush with the tip of the spout. (If the sausage meat starts to stick to the spoon, dip the spoon in ice water before continuing.) Take the funnel away from your body and pull an inch or two of casing off of the funnel and tie it. Reposition the funnel. Use the thumb and forefinger of the hand that's holding the funnel to guide the casing and shape links as you force the meat mixture down through the funnel with a wooden spoon held in your other hand (see diagram). Tie off at desired lengths as in the grinder method and continue stuffing until the casing is filled.

As we have already mentioned, you will quickly get the feel of the process and see how simple it is—and what fun. With either the grinder or the funnel-and-spoon method, two people can work as a team, with one stuffing and forcing the meat and the other guiding the casing and tying off. Or you can get a large group of people together and make several kinds of sausages during an afternoon or even a whole day. While a couple of people are working on stuffing one kind, others can be mixing up the meat and spices for the next batch, and still others can be grinding for another variety. Alone or in a group, you'll surely find sausagemaking enjoyable. And as you see the chains of delicious-smelling sausages grow, you will have to stand back and admire the "fruits" of your labor.

You will probably want to cook and eat the sausages as soon as they are ready. Or you can store them in the refrigerator for up to three or four days. Some sausages can be frozen for up to six weeks, although there will be some flavor loss due to cell breakdown. However, do not freeze sausages that have been smoked or dried.

Now the rest is up to you. Start scanning the recipe sections that begin on page 39 and select something that sounds delicious to you for your first sausagemaking attempt.

32

Smoking Sausage

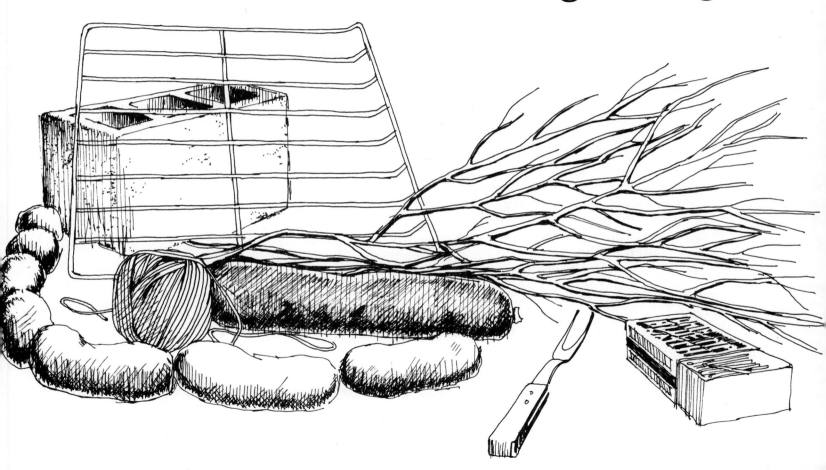

Some sausages are cooked and eaten immediately after stuffing, or used in specific recipes, while others require that special procedures be followed for preservation. The methods we have used to preserve sausages are smoking and drying. Occasionally, the meat used in your sausages will need to be brine cured before grinding. Specific instructions for drying and brine curing will be included in individual recipes. Since smoking requires special equipment and know-how, we felt it needed a section of its own.

The process of smoking meat was devised many centuries ago when few other means of preserving meats were available. Entire catches of fish or meat could be smoked and stored for use in seasons when they were scarce. Smoking procedures were refined through the years, and it became a way to enhance the flavor of food as well as preserve it.

Smoking helps dry sausages quickly, thus lessening their susceptibility to decay. The chemicals in the smoke itself impart a delicious flavor and aroma and improve the appearance and texture of some sausages. These chemicals also help to deter the growth of bacteria and to prevent the sausages from becoming rancid.

Many people have the mistaken notion that once meat is smoked, it is ready to be eaten. In fact, variations in the smoking temperature and length of smoking time are what determine whether the process actually completes the cooking of the meat or simply flavors it. The individual sausage recipes will tell you whether further cooking is necessary following smoking.

There are some well-designed smoke ovens available on the market today. They are generally well made and eliminate all guesswork from the smoking procedure, but they tend to be somewhat expensive. Before making the investment, you might like to try making your own smoke oven. This can be surprisingly easy.

34   We were able to make use of a beautiful, old, stone fireplace on our property, but equally good results can be obtained by using a covered barbecue. If you are even moderately handy, you can build a very serviceable smoke oven out of cinder blocks. A cinder block

oven needs no mortar, so you can adjust the height of the oven to accommodate a long string of sausages or even a thirty-inch kielbasa.

Whatever type of smoke oven you buy or make, remember the smoke must be kept moving freely around the meat, yet still be somewhat confined. In other words, you need a bottom and a top draft for your smoke oven to function properly. Do not enclose your meat tightly, expecting to come up with a good, smoky sausage—too much smoke can be unpalatable.

In the diagram below, we have illustrated the type of fireplace we used for our own smoke oven. It is made of fieldstone and seems to be a popular choice for outdoor cooking in many suburban areas. Since it is a fairly common type of fireplace, we thought its inclusion here would be helpful to many people.

By suspending a metal bar across the "arms" of the fireplace, we were able to make a

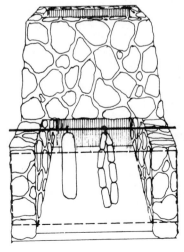

Place plywood over top opening

Dotted line indicates placement of foil

35

"hanger" for our meat without actually sinking the metal into the stone itself. By then putting a short apron of heavy-duty foil about two-thirds of the way down the front of the fireplace and a large piece of plywood over the top opening where the meat is suspended, we were able to have a good smoker with a minimum of expense and effort. The fireplace has its own chimney to provide a draft.

The diagram on the left illustrates how a covered barbecue can be used as a smoker. The sausages can be hung by their strings or by inexpensive S-hooks on the barbecue spit. This method allows all surfaces to be exposed to the smoke. Fashion a large piece of heavy-duty aluminum foil into a rectangular front panel, and secure it at the sides of the barbecue with strong masking tape so that it does not blow away. Check to make sure the smoke moves freely, and adjust the foil as needed. If more of a draft is necessary, simply poke a few small holes in the foil with a knife.

The diagram on the right shows how to "stack up" a cinder block smoke oven. You can use ordinary oven racks, or even barbecue racks, for the meat; you can also suspend a metal bar, as in the preceding example, or do both, as illustrated.

Cut plywood to partially cover the top of the smoke oven and to cover all but the lower part of the front. The number of cinder blocks needed will depend on the size of oven you decide to make; obviously, the larger the oven, the greater the expense.

Keep in mind that your smoke oven need not be restricted to sausages, but can be used to smoke anything from meats and fish to poultry, cheese, and salt. If you should decide to expand your smoking repertoire, we suggest a book by Jack Sleight and Raymond Hull, *Home Book of Smoke Cooking Meat, Fish and Game* (New York: Pyramid Books, 1976).

A slow-burning wood fire is the ideal source of fuel for a smoke oven, but you may also use charcoal sprinkled with a fine layer of sawdust. Place the wood or charcoal in an even layer in the bottom of the smoke oven. Be sure that your wood is not too dry or the fire will be too hot and burn too quickly. Light, using whatever method of starting the fire you prefer. In a half hour to forty-five minutes, or when the flames have died down and the oven is very hot, hang your sausages or place them on racks so that they will benefit most from the smoke. Hang an oven thermometer on the metal suspension bar or on the rack. For best results, sausages are smoked at a fairly low temperature, between 80° and 90° Fahrenheit, for the length of time suggested in the recipe you have chosen. Remember that the printed smoking time is relative—you may wish to increase or decrease it depending on your taste in sausage.

Add slightly damp wood or charcoal to the smoke oven as needed. The flavor of the sausages may be further enhanced, or even changed slightly, by adding young twigs from fruit or nut trees to the fire during smoking. We have tried apple, cherry, and hickory twigs with good results. To maintain a particular standard of smokiness or a particular flavor throughout subsequent batches of sausages, try keeping a small log in which you record smoking times and any additions of twigs. This way, if you happen to hit upon a magic formula for a particular flavor, you will be able to duplicate it.

When smoking has been completed, the sausages may be refrigerated or kept in a cool, dry place until ready to use. If mold appears, you may remove it with a paper towel dipped in vinegar, or you may simply remove the casing. If a sausage is only partially eaten, refrigerate the remaining portion.

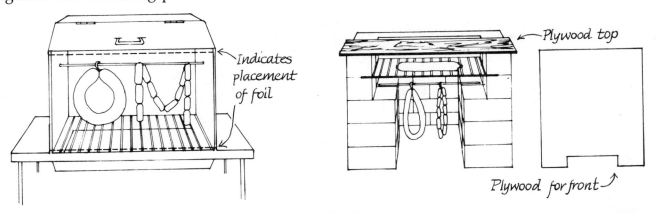

Indicates placement of foil

Plywood top

Plywood for front

37

All-Meat Sausage Recipes

We've assembled here an assortment of sausages that's sure to have something for everyone. They range from the traditional, such as bologna or liverwurst, to the exotic, such as mititei from Rumania, or Caribbean sausages made from a mixture of cold shrimp, beef, and chicken.

Before giving you the go-ahead, though, there are two things that need to be discussed, casing and saltpeter. Remember that almost all of the sausages can be formed into loaves or patties and fried, baked, broiled, or barbecued instead of being cased. Many people prefer these forms to the cased shapes.

The purpose of saltpeter in meat processing is purely aesthetic. It is not a preservative, as many people mistakenly believe, nor does it have nutritional value. It is used only to give sausages, hams, pastrami, bacon, and other meats an appetizing, rosy color. Without it, they would be a drab, ashy brown. The taste, of course, would be exactly the same, except that saltpeter does tend to toughen the meat (it is usually used with sugar in order to cut down its hardening effects).

There is concern that saltpeter may be harmful to your health. Saltpeter is a nitrate, and it is feared that nitrates convert to nitrites, both in the food itself and in our bodies. Nitrites combine with the red blood cells and, if present in sufficient quantities, they could limit the oxygen-bearing function of the hemoglobin, thereby hindering vital body processes. As we write this, both the Food and Drug Administration and the United States Department of Agriculture are still studying saltpeter, and no final decision has been reached.

Using saltpeter, then, is a matter of personal choice. If you wouldn't consider buying foods that contain it, you are not going to add it to foods that you make. We are against putting chemicals into our sausages, yet we believe that food that is pleasing to the eye is always more pleasing to the palate—and a grayish-brown homemade sausage, despite its superior ingredients, just doesn't look as good as some of the worst commercial preparations. There are two things you can do to achieve a pleasing color without using saltpeter. Either add sweet paprika in small amounts until you reach the desired color, or use

39

pure crystalline ascorbic acid. The latter is a form of Vitamin C that you can buy in a drug store. Use it at the rate of one-fourth teaspoon for every five pounds of meat mixture, to help the meat retain its natural pink color. The ascorbic acid tends to break down after a while, however, and the color will fade a bit.

If you plan to use saltpeter, you should know that it is available in drug stores. You can ask for it as "saltpeter" or by its chemical names: sodium nitrate (also called Chilean nitrate), or potassium nitrate. If you have a choice, buy potassium nitrate—it doesn't absorb as much moisture and won't toughen the meat as much.

After one or two successful attempts at sausagemaking, the color will probably no longer matter to you. The delicious taste of your own brand of sausage will by far outweigh cosmetic considerations.

In any event, we want to leave the final decision up to you. We have included saltpeter in the few recipes that seem to require it. You can use it, choose a substitute, or ignore it.

Alsatian Christmas sausage   (Yields about 3½ pounds)

To complete the Christmas tradition, wrap these sausages alternately in gold and silver foil and hang from the Christmas tree.

3 pounds lean pork
1½ pounds fatback
3 heaping tablespoons salt
¼ teaspoon ground ginger
¼ teaspoon grated nutmeg, preferably fresh

1 teaspoon sugar
1 teaspoon freshly ground black pepper
½ teaspoon cinnamon
½ teaspoon ground cloves

1. Cube the pork and fatback, mix together, and grind twice.
2. Work seasonings thoroughly into the meat mixture, using your hands.
3. Stuff into casings and tie off in 5-inch intervals.
4. Tie chains of sausages together at the ends to form circles. Dry by hanging in an airy place, at about 60° F, for at least 24 hours.
5. After drying, the sausages may be wrapped in foil as a decoration. They are usually served fried lightly in butter with a hot potato salad as a Christmas-night supper.

Basic bulk sausage   (Yields 4 pounds)

Use this in recipes calling for "sausage meat."

3 pounds lean pork
1 pound pork fat
1 teaspoon thyme
1 teaspoon basil
1 teaspoon sage

½ teaspoon cayenne
2 teaspoons freshly ground black pepper
3 teaspoons salt
1 cup chopped parsley

1. Cube the pork and fat, mix together, and grind coarsely.
2. Add the remaining ingredients and blend loosely but evenly.
3. This is a fairly open-ended recipe. Spices may be added or subtracted at will. Garlic and/or onions may be added with very good results. The pork may be replaced by veal or beef, or the meats may be used in combination.

Bayerische (Bavarian) bockwurst   *(Yields about 5 pounds)*

There are many regional varieties of bockwurst; this is one that we enjoy.

3 pounds lean veal
1½ pounds lean pork
¾ pound pork fat
1½ cups heavy cream
4 tablespoons minced chives

1 cup minced onion
½ teaspoon mace
¾ teaspoon nutmeg
2 teaspoons salt
½ teaspoon pepper

1. Cube the meats, mix together, and grind twice.
2. Cut the fat into tiny strips and combine with the meat. Put through the grinder a third time.
3. Add the remaining ingredients and blend thoroughly, using your hands.
4. Stuff into casings and tie in 4-inch links.
5. In a heavy pot or kettle, cover the sausage with *hot* water. Bring to a boil over high heat. Lower the heat to medium and simmer for 20 minutes. This bockwurst is traditionally served with mashed potatoes and sauerkraut and, naturally, bock beer.

Bologna I   *(Yields 3½ pounds)*

Saltpeter is necessary for the brine in this recipe. You can follow the recipe for Bologna II if you prefer not to use the saltpeter.

1 pound lean pork
1 pound lean veal
½ pound pork fat
½ pound finely diced bacon
4 tablespoons salt

1½ tablespoons white pepper
3 tablespoons ground ginger
2 tablespoons ground cloves
2 tablespoons sage
1½ cups white wine
saltpeter

1. Cube the meats and fat, mix together, and grind.
2. Mix in the remaining ingredients, except saltpeter, and run through the grinder a second time.
3. Stuff into broad natural casings or cheesecloth, or simply wrap with string.
4. Place in a brine of 300 parts salt water to 5 parts saltpeter for 10 days.
5. Remove from brine and hang to dry for 4 to 5 days.
6. Smoke for several hours or longer to desired flavor (see p. 34).
7. After smoking, rub casing with salad oil and hang in a cool, dry place. The bologna will keep for several months or longer. Once it has been opened, however, it should be stored in the refrigerator and eaten within 1 week.

Bologna II   *(Yields 7 pounds)*

This is a beef and pork recipe that is less time consuming than Bologna I and requires no saltpeter.

5 pounds lean beef
1½ pounds lean pork
½ pound pork fat
4 tablespoons sage
2 tablespoons sweet paprika

2 tablespoons salt
1 teaspoon cayenne
1 teaspoon freshly ground black
pepper

1. Cube the meats and fat, mix together, and grind.
2. Add seasonings and mix with your hands until well blended.
3. Stuff casings to about 2 inches thick and tie off at 10-inch intervals.
4. Place in water to cover for 1 hour.
5. Hang to dry outdoors or in a cool, dark, dry spot for several days.
6. Smoke lightly or to desired taste. Store in refrigerator and use within 2 weeks.

Boudin blanc   *(Serves 4 to 6)*

Literally "white pudding" in French, this is delicately flavored and textured.

¼ pound fatback
3 cups onions, peeled and sliced thinly
1 cup milk
⅔ cup bread crumbs
½ pound very lean, boneless veal
½ pound skinned, boned, raw breast of chicken
⅛ teaspoon allspice
⅛ teaspoon nutmeg

⅛ teaspoon ginger
⅛ teaspoon cinnamon
1 tablespoon chopped parsley
2 teaspoons salt
¼ teaspoon white pepper
1 egg
3 egg whites
½ cup heavy cream
boiling water and milk (for final cooking)

1. Cut half of the fatback into small strips. Render strips in a frying pan until you have accumulated about 3 tablespoons of fat.

44

2. Add the onions and cook very slowly, covered, for 15 minutes or until the onions are tender. Remove from heat.

3. In a small saucepan pour the milk over the bread crumbs and bring to a boil. Boil, stirring constantly, until the mixture has thickened enough to hold its shape. Set aside.

4. Cube the remaining fatback, the veal, and the chicken, mix together with the onions, and grind once. Add the allspice, nutmeg, ginger, cinnamon, parsley, salt, and pepper and grind twice more.

5. Transfer ground ingredients to a large bowl. Beat with an electric mixer for 2 minutes, add the whole egg, and beat 1 or 2 minutes more. Add the egg whites and continue to beat for 3 minutes until well blended. Blend in bread crumbs.

6. Add cream to mixture a little at a time, beating thoroughly between additions.

7. Stuff mixture into pork casings to form sausages about 5 inches long and about 1 inch thick. Refrigerate overnight.

8. Prick the boudins in several places and place on a rack in a roasting pan. Add equal parts of milk and water to cover the boudins by at least 1 inch.

9. Bring the liquid JUST to a simmer either on top of the stove or in the oven. Lower the heat slightly and poach very slowly for 25 minutes.

10. Drain the boudins, cool at room temperature, and refrigerate. Use within 3 to 4 days.

11. Boudins may be brushed with melted butter and grilled or fried. Or they may be dredged in flour and lightly fried. They are usually served with mashed potatoes.

45

Boudin noir   *(Yields 6 to 7 pounds)*

French "black pudding" is a well-seasoned blood sausage.

2 pounds chestnuts
2 teaspoons salt
1¾ cups bread crumbs
1½ cups evaporated milk
1½ cups heavy cream
3 pounds pork fat diced in tiny pieces

4 large onions, chopped
¼ cup + 2 tablespoons salt
2 teaspoons dark brown sugar
½ cup chopped parsley
1 teaspoon sage
3 quarts pig's blood
¼ cup vegetable oil

1. To prepare the chestnuts, make a cross cut on the rounded sides of the chestnuts. Roast them on a cookie sheet in a hot oven for 10 minutes. Remove shells and inner skins and place nutmeats in a pot with 2 teaspoons salt and water to cover. Simmer for 20 minutes. Cool and chop; set aside.

2. Soak the bread crumbs for 10 minutes in a mixture of the milk and the cream.

3. Brown 1 pound of the fat in a large, heavy skillet over medium heat. Add the onions and cook, stirring, until they are soft. Add the remaining fat, bread-crumb mixture, salt, sugar, parsley, and sage, and stir until well blended. Add the chestnuts and mix well. Remove to a large bowl, and blend the blood into the mixture.

4. Knot one end of the casing securely and stuff very carefully, letting the sausage fall in a single coil into a large colander or strainer. Handle this sausage gently and do not fill too tightly, since the mixture will expand somewhat.

5. Fill a large pot or kettle ⅔ full with water and bring to a boil. Remove from heat. After all signs of boiling have ceased, gently lower the colander of boudin into the water.

6. Return pot to burner, reset to very low heat. Cover and keep at the lowest possible

46

simmer for 15 minutes. Test boudin by pricking with a needle. If blood still spurts out, simmer 5 to 10 minutes longer. Remove colander from pot very carefully and place it gently into a large bowl of cold water. Soak for 5 minutes. Be extra careful at this point, since the boudin is very fragile until it is cool.

7. Spread the boudin on paper towels over several thicknesses of newspaper and use a pastry brush to glaze with the vegetable oil (a feather-type brush works well).

8. Fry or grill and serve cut in sections. These go well with fruits. In fact, you can substitute 2 pounds of McIntosh apples, stewed, for the chestnuts during preparation.

Bratwurst   (Yields 5 pounds)

Try substituting 2 teaspoons dried sage for the mace and nutmeg—delicious!

2½ pounds lean veal
2½ pounds lean pork
1½ teaspoons mace
1½ teaspoons nutmeg
3 teaspoons salt

1 teaspoon white pepper
1½ cups water
1 cup fine bread crumbs soaked in
½ cup milk

1. Cube the meats, mix together, and grind twice. Add mace, nutmeg, salt, and pepper and grind a third time.

2. Using your hands, combine the meat with the bread crumbs. Add the water and beat with a wooden spoon until light and fluffy.

3. Stuff into pork casings and tie securely into desired lengths. The bratwurst may be fried lightly in butter, but are also delicious dipped in milk and then broiled or grilled over charcoal.

47

Breakfast sausage   *(Yields about 3 pounds)*

Fry these lightly, then wrap in your favorite muffin or biscuit dough and bake. Serve with eggs for a hearty Sunday brunch.

3 pounds lean pork
3 teaspoons powdered sage
1 teaspoon summer savory
2 teaspoons marjoram
½ teaspoon nutmeg

1 tablespoon salt
2 teaspoons freshly ground black
  pepper
¼ cup water

1. Cube the pork and grind. Set aside.
2. Mix all the seasonings with the water and add to the meat, working it through until thoroughly blended.
3. Stuff into casings, tying off at 4-inch intervals. Refrigerate immediately.
4. To cook, fry slowly until cooked through and well browned on all sides.

Celebration sausage   *(Yields 1½ pounds)*

48

An elegant sausage for a special occasion. Exquisite with champagne or with a chilled white wine . . . a fine hors d'oeuvre.

1 pound lean pork
½ pound pork fat
2½ teaspoons salt
⅛ teaspoon white pepper
⅛ teaspoon cloves
⅛ teaspoon ginger

⅛ teaspoon nutmeg
⅛ teaspoon cinnamon
2½ tablespoons Madeira
2 ounces truffles, chopped
3 heaping tablespoons pistachio nuts, blanched

1. Cube the pork and fat, mix together, and grind twice. Add salt, pepper, cloves, ginger, nutmeg, and cinnamon. Mix thoroughly, using your hands.
2. Lightly blend in the Madeira, truffles, and pistachio nuts.
3. Tie off one end of a large, natural casing and stuff it firmly to form one good-sized sausage. Tie off the other end. Wrap the sausage in cheesecloth and tie with string as shown.
4. Put the sausage in a heavy pot or kettle with enough salted water to cover and bring to a boil over high heat. Lower heat to medium and simmer for 45 minutes.
5. Hang in an airy place, 55°–60° F, to cool and dry for about 2 days. After cooking, the string and cheesecloth may need a little adjusting before hanging, so tighten and straighten as needed.
6. Slice thinly and delicately and serve cold.

NOTE: This is very perishable. After the hanging period is completed, refrigerate the sausage, and be sure to use it within a week.

49

Cervelat   *(Yields 5 pounds)*

Sausage:

5 pounds lean pork
½ pound bacon, chopped
1 tablespoon chopped scallion tops
3 tablespoons chopped parsley
1 teaspoon thyme
1½ teaspoons basil
½ teaspoon ground cloves
1 teaspoon nutmeg

Cooking Liquid:

8 cups beef consomme
1 onion, sliced
1 teaspoon thyme
1 tablespoon chopped parsley
1 tablespoon salt
1 teaspoon pepper
1 teaspoon nutmeg

1. Cube the pork, mix with the bacon, and grind twice.
2. Mix in the remaining ingredients until well blended, using your hands.
3. Stuff casings until quite full, tying off at 10-inch intervals.
4. Hang in a cool, dry place for 4 days.
5. Put the stock and remaining soup ingredients in a covered pot. Bring to a boil. Add the cervelat. Reduce heat, cover, and simmer very slowly for 4 hours. Remove from stock. The cervelat can be eaten immediately, either hot or cold.

50

Čevapčići   *(Yields 2 pounds)*

A Yugoslavian specialty. We advise quadrupling this recipe and having a feast.

2 pounds lean beef round
  or
1 pound lean beef round
  plus 1 pound lean veal
3 cloves garlic, crushed

⅓ cup water, at room temperature
1½ teaspoons sweet paprika
½ teaspoon cayenne
2 heaping tablespoons chopped parsley
salt and pepper to taste

1. Cube the meat and grind twice. If you are using beef and veal, grind each one once, combine loosely, and grind together the second time.

2. Mix the meat well with the garlic and water, using your hands. Add the remaining ingredients and combine thoroughly. Let the mixture rest in the refrigerator for 1 hour.

3. With wet hands, shape the meat into sausages about 3 inches long and 1 inch thick.

4. Grill over charcoal or broil close to the source of heat until well browned. Čevapčići is served with a generous mound of chopped onions or a pickled vegetable relish.

Chaurice   *(Yields 2 30-inch sausages)*

This is a spicy Creole sausage, redolent of garlic, and truly blessed with sinus-clearing qualities.

3 pounds lean pork
¾ pound pork fat
¾ cup finely chopped onion
5 cloves garlic, crushed in 1 tablespoon water
2½ teaspoons dried hot pepper
  flakes
2 teaspoons cayenne

1½ teaspoons freshly ground black
  pepper
½ teaspoon allspice
½ teaspoon sugar
1 tablespoon salt
1 teaspoon Tabasco sauce
¾ cup chopped parsley
2 pieces pork casing, each about 1 yard long

1. Cube the pork and pork fat, mix together, and grind coarsely.
2. Place in a large bowl and add the onions, garlic, pepper flakes, cayenne, black pepper, allspice, sugar, and salt; mix well. Add the Tabasco and parsley and blend thoroughly with your hands. Let the mixture rest for ½ hour; then beat until light with a wooden spoon.
3. Tie a secure knot at one end of each casing. Fill casings to within 3 inches of open ends. Tie open ends securely with a tight knot.
4. Prick each sausage in half a dozen places with a needle. To cook, place sausages in a large pot or kettle with salted water to cover. Bring to a boil over medium-high heat; immediately lower heat to medium and simmer for 45 minutes, uncovered, until water has evaporated. Drain off most of the sausage fat from the pot and fry the sausage, turning occasionally, for 10 to 12 minutes, or until well browned. Slice and eat hot or cold, or use in Creole gumbos or jambalaya.

Chicken sausage *(Yields 2 15-inch sausages)*

4 pounds cooked white chicken meat
½ pound bacon, cooked and crumbled
¾ pound chicken livers
1 dozen eggs
1 tablespoon salt

1 teaspoon nutmeg
½ teaspoon ground cloves
½ teaspoon white pepper
6 cups finely ground cornflake crumbs
10 quarts homemade chicken stock (or use bouillon cubes in water)

1. Run the chicken and bacon through grinder. Place in a large bowl and set aside.
2. Boil chicken livers for 8 to 10 minutes, drain, mince, and place in another bowl.

3. Add 8 well-beaten eggs, salt, nutmeg, cloves, and white pepper to the livers and mix well.

4. Add liver mixture to chicken and bacon and mix well.

5. Add enough cornflake crumbs so that the mixture will hold together when you shape it.

6. Divide mixture in half and shape each half into a sausage measuring 12 to 15 inches long and 3 to 4 inches thick.

7. Break remaining eggs into a bowl or pan long enough to hold the sausages. Beat well.

8. Roll each sausage in cornflake crumbs, making sure both ends and sides are well covered. Dip in beaten egg, then in crumbs once again. Repeat.

9. Case in 3 layers of cheesecloth.

10. Plunge into boiling stock, cover, and simmer slowly for 1¾ hours.

11. Remove from stock and let stand at room temperature for 8 hours or overnight.

12. Refrigerate for at least 1 day before serving.

13. Store in refrigerator. This doesn't take particularly well to freezing.

Chorizo   *(Yields about 3 pounds)*

3 pounds lean beef round
or
1½ pounds lean beef round
plus 1½ pounds lean pork
¼ cup red wine vinegar
1 large onion, minced
3 or 4 cloves garlic, crushed
1 heaping tablespoon salt

2½ teaspoons brown sugar
½ teaspoon cumin
½ teaspoon coriander
1 teaspoon dried mint leaves
1 tablespoon oregano
1 teaspoon basil
3 tablespoons chili powder

53

1. Cube the meat and grind coarsely.
2. Combine the meat with the vinegar, onion, garlic, salt, and sugar. Add the remaining ingredients and mix with your hands until thoroughly blended. Refrigerate overnight.
3. Stuff into casings to form sausages about 1 foot long and 1 inch thick. You may also form the meat into rolls, wrap in muslin, and tie with string.
4. Hang to dry in a warm spot away from light for 2 days (a dry cellar or attic is a perfect place).
5. Remove muslin, if used. Slice the sausage into ½-inch rounds and fry lightly in olive oil. Chorizo can be used in any recipe calling for a dry, spicy sausage.

Crépinettes   *(Yields about 2½ pounds)*

large pieces of caul fat
water
1 tablespoon white vinegar
2 pounds basic bulk sausage

2 tablespoons dry red wine
¾ cup pistachio nuts, blanched
¼ pound butter, melted
1½ cups bread crumbs

1. In a bowl, cover the caul fat with a mixture of warm water and the white vinegar. Soak for 15 to 20 minutes or until pliable.
2. Using kitchen shears or ordinary scissors cut the caul fat into 4-inch squares.
3. In a medium-sized bowl, moisten the sausage meat with the wine and blend well, using your hands. Add the pistachio nuts and blend again.
4. Holding a square of the caul fat in your hand, put a large spoonful of the sausage meat in the center and wrap it like a little package, pressing the edges under firmly. Continue until all squares and filling are used.

54

5. Roll the crépinettes carefully in the butter and then in the bread crumbs, placing them on a rack over a cookie sheet as they are ready.

6. Bake the crépinettes at 350° F for 40 minutes, then broil for 5 minutes. Serve immediately.

Cuban sausage   (Yields 5 pounds)

This is a spicy sausage that goes well with traditional Spanish dishes, such as Spanish rice or paella.

4 pounds lean pork
1 pound pork fat
2 tablespoons salt
2 teaspoons freshly ground black
  pepper

5 cloves garlic, crushed
1 teaspoon cumin
2 teaspoons oregano
¾ cup Achiote*

1. Cube the pork and fat, mix together, and grind coarsely.

2. Add salt, pepper, garlic, cumin, oregano, and achiote and mix, using a wooden spoon, until well blended. Grind again.

3. Stuff pork casings to form sausages about 4 inches long and 1 inch thick. Tie off securely.

4. Prick the sausages with a needle and hang to dry for 6 hours in a cool, dry spot. Refrigerate until ready to use.

5. These sausages may be sautéed or grilled and used in soups, stews, casseroles, or sauces.

*Achiote is a coloring used in many Latin foods. It can be found in the specialty sections of some supermarkets or in a Latin grocery.

English faggots *(Yields about 2½ pounds)*

These little sausages wrapped in caul fat are so named because they look like small bundles, or faggots.

¾ pound pork liver
¾ pound pork kidney
½ pound lean pork shoulder
½ pound fatback
3 medium onions, chopped finely
2 cloves garlic, crushed
½ teaspoon sage
1 teaspoon salt

½ teaspoon freshly ground black pepper
¾ teaspoon mace
1 tablespoon vegetable oil
3 eggs, slightly beaten
3 cups soft bread crumbs
1 large piece of caul fat
3 tablespoons white vinegar
1 cup beef stock or bouillon

1. Chop the liver very finely. Slice the kidney in half and carefully remove all trace of membrane with a sharp knife. Chop the kidney very finely.

2. Cube the pork shoulder and fatback, mix together, and grind twice. Mix with the liver and kidneys.

3. Combine the meat mixture with the onions, garlic, sage, salt, pepper, and mace. Blend thoroughly, using your hands.

4. Heat the oil in a heavy skillet over medium heat. Reduce the heat to low and sauté the meat mixture for 30 minutes. Stir often to keep mixture from browning. Drain in a colander, reserving liquid.

5. Mix the meat with the eggs and bread crumbs until the mixture is very stiff.

6. Place the caul fat in a bowl of tepid water combined with the vinegar and soak for 15 to 20 minutes or until pliable.

7. When caul fat is workable, cut into 5-inch squares. Put a plump meatball of the pork mixture in the center of each square and wrap like little packages.

8. Place the faggots close together in a greased baking pan or shallow casserole. Pour the beef bouillon into the pan.

9. Place in the center of an oven, preheated to 350° F, for 30 minutes. Drain the pan juices and add them to the cooking liquid you have reserved in step 4. Refrigerate the combined liquids until the fat rises to the top.

10. Continue cooking the faggots for 30 minutes more. Raise the heat to 400° F and cook for another 10 minutes. Serve hot.

11. Skim fat from refrigerated cooking liquid, heat, and serve as gravy, if desired. The faggots can also be eaten cold or can be reheated by wrapping in foil and baking at 350° F for 30 minutes.

Escarola imbottita (escarole sausage)   (Yields about 2½ pounds)

1¼ pound Italian hot sausage, uncased
¾ pound Italian sweet sausage, uncased
2 tablespoons olive oil
2 or 3 heads escarole
3 cloves garlic, minced
1½ cups chopped black and green olives

5 tablespoons pine nuts
½ cup bread crumbs
½ teaspoon basil
1½ teaspoons oregano
6 tablespoons chopped parsley
1½ tablespoons drained capers
salt and pepper

1. Plunge the escarole into boiling water and let boil 3 to 4 minutes. Remove, refresh with cold running water. Drain and set aside.

2. In a large skillet, heat the olive oil and add the sausage meat. Cook over medium-low heat until nicely browned.

3. Increase the heat and start adding the remaining ingredients, stirring constantly. Make sure that all ingredients are spread evenly throughout. Remove from heat when well blended and cooked through.

4. Prepare the sausages as follows: Using only the largest leaves of the escarole, lay 2 leaves down and overlap them by about 2 inches. Spoon some of the sausage mixture onto the leaves. Fold the whole thing into a little bundle and tie with string wrapped vertically and horizontally, as for a package. Rub each sausage with a small amount of olive oil.

5. Simmer in beef stock, covered, for ½ hour.

Frankfurters   (Yields 7½ pounds)

If you prefer all-beef franks, substitute beef for the pork, and use beef fat rather than pork fat.

2½ pounds lean beef
2½ pounds lean pork
2½ pounds pork fat
1½ cups flour
5 tablespoons coriander
1¾ teaspoons mace

1½ teaspoons cayenne
1 teaspoon garlic powder
4 tablespoons salt
2 teaspoons sugar
⅓ cup minced onion
2½ cups cold water

1. Cube the meats and fat, mix together, and grind coarsely.
2. Sift together the flour, coriander, mace, cayenne, garlic powder, salt, and sugar.
3. Add the flour mixture, onion, and water to the meat and mix, using your hands, until thoroughly blended. Grind once or twice more to make a fine-textured sausage.

4. Stuff into natural or muslin casings to desired plumpness, tying off at 3-inch intervals for cocktail wieners and at 6-inch intervals for standard franks.

5. The frankfurters can either be smoked or precooked. *To smoke,* hang for 4 or 5 hours until they are a rich reddish brown. *To precook,* place in a deep kettle with water to cover and bring to a boil. Lower heat and simmer 8 to 10 minutes or until they rise to the surface. Drain and rinse with cold water. When cool, hang until dry.

6. Refrigerate the franks you will eat within a few days and freeze the rest.

7. Franks may be eaten cold, boiled, grilled, or fried. If boiling, cook for about 10 minutes. If grilling or frying, cook to desired doneness.

French garlic sausage *(Yields 3¾ pounds)*

This is good as an hors d'oeuvre, and it is a fine sausage for cassoulet.

3 pounds lean pork	¼ teaspoon nutmeg
¾ pound fatback, diced in tiny pieces	¼ teaspoon cloves
3½ tablespoons salt	¼ teaspoon cinnamon
1 teaspoon freshly ground black pepper	4 cloves garlic, crushed
⅛ teaspoon cayenne	1½ teaspoons whole black peppercorns
	2 tablespoons brandy

1. Cube the pork and grind twice.
2. Add salt, ground pepper, cayenne, nutmeg, cloves, cinnamon, and garlic. Mix thoroughly, using your hands, and grind once more.
3. Lightly mix fatback with meat mixture. Add peppercorns alternately with brandy

until evenly blended. Take your time with this step, since even blending is very important to the flavor of this sausage.

4. Stuff the mixture firmly into large casings to form 1 or 2 thick sausages.

5. Hang to dry in an airy place, about 60° F, for at least 4 days. Store in the refrigerator and use within 1 week. This sausage is delicious broiled, or sliced and fried lightly in butter.

French liver sausage   *(Yields 4½ pounds)*

A fine variety of liver sausage; worth the extra effort involved.

Brine:
- 6 cups water
- ⅛ cup baking soda
- 2½ pounds unadulterated rock salt
- 1 cup dark brown sugar
- 1 teaspoon juniper berries
- a tiny sliver of nutmeg
- 1 bay leaf
- 1 teaspoon whole black peppercorns
- 2 whole cloves

Sausage:
- 1½ pounds leg of pork, salted in brine
- 1½ pounds pork liver
- 1½ pounds fatback
- 3 tablespoons butter
- 4 onions, chopped
- ½ cup kirsch
- 3 tablespoons salt
- 2 teaspoons freshly ground black pepper
- ¼ teaspoon nutmeg
- ¼ teaspoon cloves
- ¼ teaspoon cinnamon

Brine:
1. Bring to a boil the water, baking soda, rock salt, and brown sugar.
2. Meanwhile, place the juniper berries, nutmeg, bay leaf, peppercorns, and cloves on a small square of muslin or doubled cheesecloth and tie in a little bundle with clean, white string or thread.
3. Skim the foam from the boiling mixture and remove from heat. Put the bag of spices into the hot liquid and leave in the pot until cool.
4. Clean a large bowl or crock with boiling water and baking soda. When the brine mixture is actually COLD, remove the bag of spices and strain the liquid through cheesecloth into the bowl or crock.
5. Put the piece of pork into the liquid so that it is completely immersed. If necessary, weight the meat with a dish to keep it below the surface. Soak for 3 days in a cool place, away from direct light.

Sausage:
1. Grind the liver 3 times. (If you have a blender, chop the liver in a few pieces and puree.)
2. Chop the pork and fat coarsely and grind together.
3. Melt the butter in an iron skillet and cook the onions slowly, mashing occasionally with a fork, until soft and mushy. Cool.
4. Blend the onions with the liver and pork. Add the kirsch and remaining spices and mix well, using your hands.
5. Stuff into casings, tying off in 5- to 6-inch links. Hang to dry in a cool, airy place for 2 days.
6. Put the sausages in a heavy pot of boiling water. Lower heat and simmer gently for 1 hour. Prick sausages with a needle as they rise to the surface.
7. Drain and cool. Serve fried lightly in butter. This is good with fried potatoes and fruit, especially apples.

61

Gehirnwurst   *(Yields about 4 pounds)*

This is a highly perishable sausage and should be used only when completely fresh.

2½ pounds pork brains
2½ tablespoons vinegar
¾ pound lean pork
¾ pound pork fat

1½ tablespoons salt
1 teaspoon freshly ground black pepper
1 teaspoon mace

1. Bring salted water to boil, add the pork brains and vinegar, cover, and simmer for 20 minutes.
2. Drain the brains, place them in a large bowl, and mash with a fork. Set aside.
3. Grind the pork and pork fat and add to the brains, blending carefully and thoroughly.
4. Add the salt, pepper, and mace and mix thoroughly.
5. Stuff into casings, tying off at 4- to 5-inch intervals.
6. Bring 2 quarts of water to a boil, add sausages, reduce heat, and poach for 10 to 12 minutes.
7. Cool and keep refrigerated until ready to cook.
8. To cook, sauté slowly in butter or margarine.

Gogue   *(Makes 2 to 3 medium or 1 large sausage)*

This is a "boudin blanc et noir," or black and white pudding, made in France for the Christmas holidays.

2½ pounds beet leaves	3 quarts + ¼ cup pig's blood
6 tablespoons oil	1 quart + 1 cup heavy cream
1¼ cups finely chopped onion	3 eggs, beaten
2 heaping tablespoons salt	1 teaspoon sugar
½ teaspoon white pepper	⅛ teaspoon allspice
¾ cup bread crumbs	large pork casings
1 cup milk	

1. Wash the beet leaves, drain, and set aside to dry. Cut in pieces.
2. Heat 2 tablespoons oil in a heavy skillet and quickly sauté the beet leaves until just tender. Drain.
3. In a blender, make a smooth, dry puree of the beet leaves. Set aside.
4. Heat 3 tablespoons oil in a heavy skillet and cook the onion slowly until it becomes mushy, stirring often. Add the remaining tablespoon of oil to the pan and when it has heated, stir in the beet-leaf puree. Blend in salt and pepper and cook over low heat, stirring occasionally, for 10 minutes.
5. Place bread crumbs in a small bowl. Cover with milk and allow to soak.
6. Meanwhile, pour the blood into a large bowl. Add the cream, eggs, sugar and allspice. Stir, do not beat, with a wire whisk.
7. Blend the bread-crumb mixture into the blood mixture. Finally, add the onion-beet mixture and blend well.
8. Tie one end of the casing very securely and ladle the filling into the open end. This can be clumsy if you are making the sausage alone; you may find it easier to make 2 or 3

63

smaller sausages rather than 1 large one. Whichever you make, do not fill too tightly. Knot the open end securely.

9. Place the gogue in water that is barely simmering and poach gently for 35 minutes. Drain and allow to dry.

10. Hang in a cool, dry place for 4 days before eating. To cook, slice and fry quickly in butter.

Guatemalan morango   *(Yields about 15 sausages)*

We got this recipe from a Guatemalan friend who had done a bit of butchering back home.

1 pound pork
½ pound pork fat
1 quart pork blood
4 tablespoons chopped parsley
4 tablespoons chopped fresh coriander

4 tablespoons chopped fresh mint
3 sweet or hot peppers, finely chopped
6 large onions, finely chopped

1. Cube the pork and pork fat, mix together, and grind coarsely.
2. Add pork blood, parsley, coriander, and mint, and thoroughly blend.
3. Add peppers and onions and mix thoroughly.
4. Stuff into casings, tying off at 6-inch intervals.
5. To cook, boil first for about 5 minutes, then fry until well browned.

64

For GUATEMALAN LONGANIZA use the same ingredients as in Guatemalan morango, omitting the blood. Follow the same method of preparation.   *(Makes about 15 sausages)*

Haitian sausage   *(Yields 3½ pounds)*

This was unlike any other sausage we had encountered. The surprising combination of ingredients complement each other beautifully.

1 pound raw shrimp, shelled and cleaned
½ pound boiled ham
2 pounds lean beef
1 cup minced onion
3 large cloves garlic, crushed
2 tablespoons hot red pepper flakes

½ teaspoon cayenne
1 tablespoon salt
1 teaspoon freshly ground black pepper
3 eggs
2 cups dry bread crumbs
2 medium onions, sliced
2 medium-sized bay leaves

1. Chop the shrimp and ham and set aside in a large bowl.
2. Cube the beef and grind coarsely. Add to the shrimp-and-ham mixture and mix loosely.
3. Using your hands, thoroughly combine the meat mixture with the onion and garlic. Add the pepper flakes, cayenne, salt, and black pepper and mix again.
4. Grind the entire mixture together once.
5. Beat one of the eggs well with a fork. Add ½ cup of the bread crumbs to the beaten egg and stir well. Add to the meat and blend well. Shape into 2 or 3 large sausages.
6. Beat the remaining 2 eggs with 1 tablespoon water and pour into a bowl or pan long enough to hold the sausages.
7. Roll the sausages first in the beaten eggs and then in the remaining bread crumbs, pressing down firmly to coat. Repeat, if desired.
8. Place the sausages on a large rectangle of unbleached muslin or on a double thickness of cheesecloth, wrap, and tie securely with clean, white string.

9. Fill a large, heavy kettle with salted water and bring to a boil over high heat. Add the sliced onion and the bay leaves and boil 5 minutes more.

10. Lower the sausages into the boiling water very carefully. When water returns to a boil, lower the heat and simmer gently, covered, for 1 hour. If necessary, add water to keep sausages covered.

11. Remove sausages and let cool. When completely cooled, unwrap, slice, and serve cold with a salad.

Helena Troy's sausage   *(Yields 5 pounds)*

Our friend Jim was the only sausagemaker we knew until we started making sausages ourselves. He credits his mother with this cheesey sausage, which they make in 20-pound quantities and freeze. We've adapted a 5-pound version. Use our proportions or adapt the ingredients to your own taste.

5 pounds pork butt or shoulder	2 tablespoons fennel seeds
4 teaspoons garlic powder	1 tablespoon salt
2 tablespoons oregano	1 teaspoon black pepper
2 tablespoons chopped parsley	½ cup grated Romano cheese
1 teaspoon thyme	

1. Cube the pork and grind coarsely.

2. Place in a large bowl and blend in spices and cheese, using your hands. (If you want hot sausage, add hot pepper flakes to taste at this point.)

3. Stuff into casings, tying off at 4-inch intervals.

4. To cook, boil in water to cover for about 5 minutes. Drain off water, then fry in same pan until nicely browned on all sides and cooked through.

Irish pork sausage   *(Yields about 2 pounds)*

A combination of herbs that blend beautifully. These sausages are a special treat when served with "Boxty," an Irish potato pancake (see recipe on p. 148).

1 pound lean pork	1½ teaspoons salt
½ pound pork fat	1 teaspoon thyme
2¼ cups soft bread crumbs	1 teaspoon basil
1 egg plus one egg white, lightly beaten	¾ teaspoon rosemary
	1 teaspoon marjoram
2 cloves garlic, crushed or minced	¾ teaspoon freshly ground black pepper

1. Dice the pork and fat, mix together, and grind coarsely. Blend in the bread crumbs.
2. Add the egg and garlic and mix thoroughly, using your hands. Add the remaining ingredients and mix again.
3. Form the mixture into sausage shapes about 1 inch think and 3 to 4 inches long.
4. Sauté the sausages in butter or a light oil in a heavy skillet until well browned. Drain and serve hot.

Italian fennel sausage   *(Yields 5 pounds)*

Omit the hot pepper for a milder sausage.

5 pounds pork
1 tablespoon salt
2 tablespoons freshly ground
  black pepper

1 tablespoon fennel seeds
½ teaspoon hot red pepper flakes
  (more or less, to taste)
2 tablespoons chopped parsley

1. Cube the meat and grind coarsely.
2. Add the remaining ingredients and mix thoroughly, using your hands.
3. Stuff into casings, tying off at 3-inch intervals. Store in refrigerator for no more than
3 or 4 days, or freeze.
4. To cook, boil for several minutes in water to cover, then simmer or fry until well
browned.

Italian hot sausage   *(Yields about 3½ pounds)*

Have lots of cold drinks ready before biting into these.

3 pounds lean pork
½ pound lean beef
1 pound pork fat
12 cloves garlic, minced
3 teaspoons crushed red pepper
2 teaspoons fennel seeds
½ teaspoon thyme
4 finely crumbled bay leaves

4 teaspoons salt
1¼ teaspoons freshly ground black
  pepper
½ teaspoon nutmeg
½ teaspoon coriander
2 teaspoons sweet paprika
  (optional; it's just for color)
½ cup water

1. Cube the meats and fat, mix together, and grind.
2. Add the remaining ingredients and thoroughly blend, using your hands.
3. Stuff into pork casings, tying off at 4- to 5-inch intervals.
4. Cover and wrap tightly. Freeze or store in refrigerator. If stored in refrigerator, be sure to cook within 3 days.
5. To cook, boil in water to cover for about 5 minutes. Drain off the water and fry the sausages in their own fat until nicely browned and cooked through. Prick casings several times with a fork to prevent popping.

Italian sweet sausage   *(Yields about 5 pounds)*

Cook these in tomato sauce with Italian hot sausages and serve with homemade gnocchi for a real treat.

3½ pounds lean pork	2 tablespoons basil
½ pound lean beef	2 tablespoons chopped parsley
½ pound veal	1 tablespoon salt
1½ pounds pork fat	1 tablespoon pepper
6 large cloves garlic, minced	1 teaspoon nutmeg
2 bay leaves, finely crumbled	1 teaspoon thyme

1. Cube the meats and fat, mix together, and grind.
2. Add the remaining ingredients and mix thoroughly, using your hands.
3. Stuff into casings, tying off at 3-inch intervals. Store in refrigerator for no more than 3 or 4 days, or freeze.
4. To cook, boil for several minutes in water to cover, then simmer or fry until well browned.

69

Jewish garlic sausage   *(Yields about 3 dozen sausages)*

Equally good, though no longer Jewish, made with equal parts of pork, beef, and veal.

2 pounds ground beef
2 medium onions, grated
2 eggs, beaten with a small amount
   of water
¼ cup cold water
2 small carrots, grated

6 to 8 cloves garlic, minced
2 tablespoons chopped parsley
salt and pepper
fine matzo meal
vegetable oil

1. In a bowl, mix meat, onions, and beaten eggs.
2. Add grated carrots, garlic, parsley, and water. Mix until thoroughly blended. Add salt and pepper to taste.
3. Form into tiny sausages about ¾ inch thick and 3 inches long.
4. Roll each sausage in matzo meal and fry in a little oil until nicely browned on all sides.

Kielbasa   *(Yields 3 30-inch sausages)*

70

There are many recipes for this Polish specialty. After trying several, we found this one to be our favorite.

4 pounds boneless pork shoulder	4 or 5 cloves garlic, crushed with 1 tablespoon water
1 pound shin beef or	½ teaspoon sugar
1 pound lean veal	1 tablespoon marjoram
2 heaping tablespoons salt	½ teaspoon allspice
1½ teaspoons freshly ground black pepper	1 tablespoon caraway seeds
	3 pieces of pork casing, each about 1 yard long

1. Cube the meats but do not mix together. Put the meats into separate bowls and sprinkle each with 1 tablespoon of the salt. Toss, and set aside in a cool, not cold, place for 24 hours.

2. Grind the pork coarsely. Grind the beef or veal twice, very finely.

3. Combine the meats and add the pepper, garlic, and sugar. Knead the mixture until it is thoroughly blended. Add the marjoram, allspice, and caraway seeds and beat with a wooden spoon until light and fluffy.

4. Knot each casing about 2 inches from one end. Fill each casing to within 2 inches of the open end, being careful not to fill too tightly. Knot the open end carefully. The kielbasa may be cooked immediately, or stored 4 to 5 days in coldest part of your refrigerator.

5. To cook, prick the sausage in 6 or 7 places with a needle, and put in a heavy pot with water to cover. Since this is such a large sausage, you may have to curl it gently until it fits the pot. Bring the water to a simmering point over medium heat, lower heat, and simmer, uncovered, for 40 minutes. If you do not have a large enough pot, you may put the kielbasa on a rack in a roasting pan, with water to cover, and bake it at 350° F until the water has evaporated.

6. Traditionally, kielbasa is sliced into rounds and fried in a little vegetable oil. It is then served with sauerkraut and boiled potatoes.

Knackwurst   *(Yields 5 pounds)*

Knackwurst is simply a big, fat frankfurter; there are only subtle differences between the two.

2 pounds lean beef	1 tablespoon coriander
2 pounds lean pork	1 teaspoon mace
1 pound pork fat	2½ tablespoons salt
4 cloves garlic, crushed in 1 table- spoon water	2 teaspoons sugar
½ cup minced onion	1 cup water

1. Cube the meats and fat, mix together, and grind coarsely.
2. Knead the garlic and onions into the meat mixture. Add coriander, mace, salt, sugar, and water, and mix thoroughly, using your hands. Grind again.
3. Stuff into casing to form links 5 to 6 inches long and about 1½ inches thick. Tie off securely.
4. Hang to smoke for 4 or 5 hours, or precook.
5. To precook, place knackwurst in a heavy kettle with water to cover. Bring to a boil over high heat. Lower heat to medium and simmer for 10 minutes. Drain and rinse with cold water. When cool, hang to dry. Refrigerate until ready to use, but no more than 3 to 4 days. In adapting knackwurst to recipes for frankfurters, remember that the knackwurst will have a stronger garlic flavor.

Liverwurst   *(Yields 1½ pounds)*

Also called leberwurst, this is America's favorite: a few slices on pumpernickel bread . . . ecstasy.

½ pound lean pork	½ teaspoon salt
1 small onion, peeled	½ teaspoon white pepper
½ pound pork liver	¼ teaspoon allspice
½ pound fat bacon	1 or 2 truffles, chopped (optional)

1. Put the pork in a pot with salted water to cover. Add the onion, cover, and bring to a boil over high heat. Lower the heat to medium and simmer for 30 minutes.

2. Chop the liver very finely and press through a sieve. Chop the pork as finely as you possibly can. Dice the bacon into tiny pieces. Mix the liver, pork, and bacon together.

3. Add the salt, pepper, allspice, and truffles to the meats and mix thoroughly, using your hands.

4. Fill a large casing and tie the ends securely. Drop very carefully into boiling water to cover. Lower the heat immediately. Simmer very slowly and gently for 30 minutes.

5. Wipe the sausage and hang to dry in a cool place. As soon as it is dry, refrigerate until ready to use. Use within 4 days.

Liulia   *(Serves 6)*

Served on skewers, this is known as "liulia-kebab" in Armenia. The aroma is as intoxicating as the taste.

3 pounds lean lamb	3 teaspoons salt
¾ cup finely chopped onion	⅔ cup chopped fresh mint leaves (or
3 large cloves garlic, crushed	⅓ cup dried)
1 teaspoon freshly ground black pepper	

1. Cube the lamb and grind twice.
2. Combine the lamb, onions, garlic, pepper, and salt in a large bowl. Using your hands, mix until thoroughly blended. Add mint and mix again.
3. Divide the mixture into 12 parts. With moist hands, shape each section into a 4-inch sausage, 1½ to 2 inches thick. Thread lengthwise on long skewers, leaving a small space between each sausage.
4. Broil about 4 inches from the source of heat, turning regularly until nicely browned—about 10 minutes for pink lamb and about 15 minutes for well done. If you are broiling the liulia in an oven, preheat the broiler for about 15 minutes. This sausage is delicious barbecued. It is traditionally served with whole scallions and pilaf.

Lyon sausage   *(Yields about 5 pounds)*

You can add about ½ pound of lean beef to the pork—it will speed up the drying process without affecting the taste. Don't try to eat this sausage after 4 months. The sausage will not be spoiled, but the drying will have made it much too tough to bite into.

4½ pounds lean pork
1½ teaspoons salt
1½ teaspoons pepper
¼ pound dried pork fat or salt
   pork, finely diced

12 whole white peppercorns
4 large cloves garlic, crushed
1 extra-large pork casing

1. Cube the pork and grind.
2. Add salt, pepper, and dried pork fat, and thoroughly blend.

3. Add peppercorns and garlic and mix through.
4. Using your hands, knead the mixture, continuing for 15 minutes, or even longer.
5. Stuff the hog casing, tying off at 10- to 18-inch intervals. These are very large, heavy sausages.
6. Hang in a cool, dry place for 1 week.
7. Wrap completely around, width and length, with string to prevent any curving during drying. The sausage should be as straight as possible.
8. Hang again in cool, dry place for about 3 months before eating. Store in refrigerator after opening and eat within 1 week.

Mettwurst   *(Yields 1½ pounds)*

A tasty sandwich spread that's a nice change from liverwurst. In Germany, it's one of a number of sausages called schmierwurst, meaning it can be smeared or spread.

½ pound lean pork	1 teaspoon salt
½ pound pork liver	½ teaspoon white pepper
½ pound pork fat	½ teaspoon coriander

1. Put pork in a pot with salted water to cover. Bring to a boil, lower heat and simmer, covered, for ½ hour. Drain off water and cool.
2. Chop the liver very finely and press through a sieve.
3. Cube the pork and pork fat, mix with the liver, and grind several times until smooth and pasty.
4. Add salt, pepper, and coriander and blend well.

75

5. Fill a large casing with all of the mixture, tying off each end securely.

6. Drop carefully into boiling water to cover. Reduce heat and simmer slowly for 20 minutes.

7. Hang to dry for a couple of days in a cool, dry place. Smoke lightly. The sausage is now ready to use. Store it in the refrigerator; it doesn't freeze well.

Midwest farmhouse sausage   (Yields about 2 pounds)

This is a spicy and meaty sausage, delicious with waffles and maple syrup for breakfast or with home-fried potatoes for a good country supper.

2 pounds lean pork shoulder	1 teaspoon thyme
½ cup finely chopped onion	1 teaspoon basil
1½ teaspoons minced garlic	2 teaspoons salt
2 tablespoons chopped parsley	1 teaspoon freshly ground black
2 tablespoons sage	pepper
1 teaspoon marjoram	2 tablespoons butter
1 teaspoon cayenne	2 tablespoons vegetable oil

1. Cube the pork and grind very finely. Mix with the onion, garlic, and parsley.

2. Combine the sage, marjoram, cayenne, thyme, basil, salt, and pepper. Knead the spice mixture into the meat until evenly blended.

3. Beat the mixture with a wooden spoon until light and fluffy. Let it rest ½ hour in the refrigerator.

4. Cut a large piece of waxed paper and form a large, thick sausage on it with the meat

76

mixture. Wrap tightly and refrigerate for at least 3 hours or overnight. Or stuff into casings, tying off in 3-inch links.

5. In a heavy skillet, melt the butter in the oil over medium heat. Slice the large sausage into ½-inch thick rounds immediately before cooking. Fry for 4 minutes on each side. Drain and serve.

Missouri pork sausage   *(Yields 2½ pounds)*

2½ pounds pork, not too lean
1 tablespoon salt
2 teaspoons freshly ground black
  pepper

½ teaspoon cinnamon
¼ teaspoon cayenne
¼ teaspoon nutmeg
¼ cup sage

1. Cube the pork and grind coarsely.
2. Add the salt, pepper, cinnamon, cayenne, and nutmeg to the meat and mix well. Add the sage and knead it into the meat mixture.
3. You may follow any of the following procedures:
Refrigerate the meat mixture, as is, for 8 hours or overnight. Shape into patties about 3 inches in diameter and about ½ inch thick.
    or
Cut a piece of waxed paper the length of the sausage you wish to make; form the meat into a large, thick sausage on the waxed paper, wrap it tightly, and refrigerate overnight. Slice into rounds about ½ inch thick.
    or
Stuff into casings, tying off in 3-inch links.

4. Heat a large, heavy skillet, preferably iron, over moderate heat. Fry the sausages in their own fat, turning frequently, for 10 to 12 minutes. If the meat is particularly lean, add a small amount of vegetable oil to the skillet. Drain and serve.

Mititei   *(Yields 2 pounds)*

A delicious Rumanian sausage; good with black bread spread with sweet butter and topped with sliced radishes.

2 pounds lean beef round
3 cloves garlic, crushed or minced
1 teaspoon baking soda
2 teaspoons salt

1 teaspoon freshly ground black pepper
½ cup warm water
⅓ cup chopped parsley
¼ cup olive oil

1. Cube the beef and grind twice.
2. Mix together the garlic, baking soda, salt, pepper, and water and thoroughly blend with the meat. Add the parsley and mix well with your hands.
3. With moist hands, form sausages about 3 inches long and about ¾ inch thick. Refrigerate the sausages for 1 hour.
4. Brush the sausages with olive oil. Grill over hot coals or broil in a preheated oven, turning often, until nicely browned.

Moroccan lamb sausage   *(Serves 6)*

These are delicious with a dipping sauce of plain yogurt.

3 pounds lean lamb
1 cup chopped parsley
1 cup minced onion
1 teaspoon marjoram
¼ teaspoon cumin
¾ teaspoon coriander

1 teaspoon oregano
1 teaspoon cayenne
1 teaspoon freshly ground black
pepper
1 teaspoon salt

1. Cube the lamb and grind coarsely.
2. Add the parsley and onion and mix well. Add the remaining ingredients and thoroughly blend, using your hands. Grind again.
3. Divide the mixture into 12 parts. With moist hands, shape each section into a sausage about 1½ to 2 inches thick and about 4½ inches long. Thread lengthwise on skewers leaving about ½ inch between sausages.
4. Broil or barbecue about 4 inches from the source of heat, turning often, until nicely browned—about 10 minutes for pink lamb and about 15 minutes for well done.
5. Serve hot with pilaf or with cucumbers in yogurt.

Norwegian sausage   *(Yields about 4 pounds)*

Delicious served cold, or sautéed in butter.

2½ pounds lean flank steak
1¼ pounds lean pork
1½ tablespoons salt
2 to 3 medium onions, grated

2½ teaspoons freshly ground black
    pepper
1½ teaspoons nutmeg

1. Cube the flank steak and pork, mix together, and grind.
2. Add salt, onion, pepper, and nutmeg and thoroughly blend.
3. Stuff into casings, tying off at 4-inch intervals.
4. Simmer in salted water to cover for about ½ hour.
5. Drain, cool, and store in refrigerator. Use within 3 to 4 days.

Parisian saucisson   *(Yields 6 pounds)*

6 pounds lean pork
5 tablespoons salt
3½ teaspoons freshly ground black
    pepper

2½ teaspoons pimiento, finely
    minced
½ teaspoon sweet paprika
butter

1. Cube the pork and grind.
2. Add the remaining ingredients and thoroughly blend, using your hands.
3. Stuff into casings, tying off at 8- to 10-inch intervals.
4. To cook, nearly fill a skillet with water and bring to a rolling boil. Remove from heat, add saucisson, and cover. Let stand for 10 to 15 minutes. Drain off water. Sauté in butter until nicely browned on all sides and cooked through.

Pennsylvania Dutch sausage   *(Yields about 6 pounds)*

4 pounds lean pork
1 pound fatback
6½ tablespoons sage
2 tablespoons ground cloves

2½ tablespoons coriander
5 tablespoons salt
2½ teaspoons pepper

1. Cube the pork and fatback, mix together, and grind.
2. Crush the remaining ingredients together by placing them between 2 sheets of waxed paper and going over with a rolling pin or by using mortar and pestle.
3. Add the crushed seasonings to the meat and thoroughly blend, using your hands.
4. Stuff into casings, tying off at 4-inch intervals.
5. Hang outdoors or in an open window for 24 hours, to increase flavor.
6. To cook, fry in a skillet containing a small amount of water, pricking sausages so that some fat will run off, until nicely browned and cooked through.

Polish blood sausage   *(Serves 4 to 6)*

2 cups water
½ cup pearl barley
½ pound pork fat, finely diced
2 quarts pig's blood
½ teaspoon ginger
1 teaspoon allspice

1 teaspoon freshly ground black
  pepper
1 tablespoon salt
1 clove garlic, crushed
flour
2 teaspoons baking powder

1. Boil water.
2. Place barley in a saucepan, cover with boiling water, and simmer, covered, for 15 minutes. Drain and cool.
3. In a large bowl, mix the barley with the pork fat. Add the blood, ginger, allspice, pepper, salt, and garlic. Mix well, adding enough flour to thicken to batter consistency. Stir in baking powder.
4. Make casings from strong, closely woven muslin. They will need to be ¾ filled, so judge the casing sizes by the volume of your mixture. Sew one end securely closed to form sacks.
5. Fill the sacks ¾ full and tie the open end tightly, leaving room for expansion.
6. Place the sacks carefully in boiling, salted water and simmer 1½ to 2 hours over medium heat.
7. Serve hot with butter and maple or fruit syrup.

Puerto Rican turkey and ham sausage   *(Yields 4 10-inch sausages)*

1 small (10 to 12 pound) turkey	½ teaspoon cayenne
¾ pound boiled ham	½ teaspoon dry mustard
10 eggs	½ teaspoon freshly ground black
1 pound fresh mushrooms, sliced	pepper
1 tablespoon salt	1 cup seasoned bread crumbs
1 teaspoon nutmeg	chicken or turkey stock

1. Remove skin and meat from turkey. Run through the fine blade of a grinder.
2. Mix the turkey with the ham, grind together, and place in a large bowl.
3. Add 8 of the eggs, one at a time, making sure to beat each one in well.

4. Add mushrooms, salt, nutmeg, cayenne, dry mustard, and pepper. Blend well, adding enough bread crumbs so that the mixture will hold together when you shape it.

5. Shape into 4 sausages, each 8 to 10 inches long and 2 to 3 inches thick.

6. Break remaining eggs into a bowl or pan long enough to hold the sausages. Beat the eggs well.

7. Roll the sausages first in the beaten eggs and then in bread crumbs, making sure both ends and sides are well covered.

8. Case in 3 layers of cheesecloth.

9. Plunge into boiling stock and simmer, covered, for 1 hour.

10. Remove from stock and cool at room temperature.

11. Store in refrigerator at least 24 hours before serving. Do *not* freeze.

Reindeer sausage   *(Yields just under 7 pounds)*

You may substitute venison, elk, or other game for the reindeer in this recipe.

6 pounds reindeer meat
¾ pound beef suet, kept as cold as possible
⅓ cup smoked salt
3 teaspoons table salt
1 tablespoon sage

1 teaspoon allspice
2 heaping tablespoons sugar
1 teaspoon coriander
1½ teaspoons whole mustard seeds
3 cloves garlic, crushed
3 tablespoons whole peppercorns

1. Cube the meat and suet, mix together, and grind coarsely.

2. Add the remaining ingredients to the meat and mix thoroughly. Grind twice more. Refrigerate overnight.

3. Mix thoroughly again, using your hands. Stuff into casings, tying off in 4- or 5-inch links.

4. Drop the sausages carefully into boiling water and cook until they float, about 30 minutes. Remove from the water and drain.

5. The sausages may be eaten immediately or lightly fried. Wrap unused sausage well and freeze.

Rosemary sausage   *(Yields 3 pounds)*

3 pounds lean pork shoulder
1 teaspoon salt
¾ teaspoon freshly ground black pepper

1½ teaspoons sage
3 cloves garlic, crushed in 1 tablespoon water
2 teaspoons dried rosemary

1. Trim meat well, cube, and grind coarsely.
2. Add salt, pepper, sage, garlic, and rosemary and mix well, using your hands.
3. Stuff into casings, keeping the sausages small and thin—about 3½ inches long and about ¾ inch thick. Store in refrigerator and use within 3 to 4 days.
4. Cook the sausages in butter in a heavy skillet until well browned and cooked through. Serve hot.

Saucisson au foie de volaille *(Serves 8 as an hors d'oeuvre)*

¾ cup chicken fat
¾ cup minced onions
3 cups chicken livers, cleaned and halved
⅛ teaspoon white pepper
pinch savory
pinch cinnamon
⅛ teaspoon sage

⅛ teaspoon nutmeg
⅛ teaspoon thyme
½ teaspoon salt
½ cup cognac
¾ cup soft bread crumbs
⅓ cup butter, preferably sweet, softened
⅓ cup cream cheese, softened

1. In a skillet, melt chicken fat over medium heat and sauté the onions for 10 minutes.
2. Add chicken livers, pepper, savory, cinnamon, sage, nutmeg, thyme, and salt. Sauté, stirring constantly, for 3 minutes.
3. Add the cognac, bring to a simmer, and ignite with a match. Flame for 30 seconds. Cover pan to extinguish flames and remove from heat.
4. Combine liver mixture with bread crumbs. Work in butter and cheese using a wooden spoon.
5. Grind the entire mixture.
6. Form into 1 or 2 sausage shapes and roll tightly in foil or waxed paper. Refrigerate until firm. Use sliced as an hors d'oeuvres, or as a spread. This sausage may also be enclosed in a crust and baked, or rolled in chopped pistachio nuts or other goodies, as you wish.

Schwabischewurst   *(Yields 4½ pounds)*

A German wurst that goes well with apples.

3 pounds lean pork shoulder
1½ pounds fatback
3 heaping tablespoons salt
2½ teaspoons freshly ground black pepper

1 teaspoon sugar
3 cloves garlic, crushed in 2 tablespoons water
1 tablespoon caraway seeds

1. Dice the pork and fatback, mix together, and sprinkle evenly with the salt, pepper, and sugar.

2. Grind very finely, repeating until the mixture is reduced to a fine paste.

3. Work the garlic and water to a smooth pulp; stir in the caraway seeds. Knead the garlic and caraway seeds into the meat mixture, using your hands, until evenly blended. Put through the grinder once more.

4. Fill large casings to desired size and tie off ends. Put the sausage into a heavy pot with water to cover. Bring to a boil over high heat; lower the heat and simmer for 40 minutes, partly covered. Drain, slice in thick chunks, and serve. This sausage can also be smoked.

Shrimp and lobster sausage   *(Yields about 3½ pounds)*

Try experimenting with other fish and shellfish for variety. These are a great addition to a clambake.

6 cups water
2 cloves garlic, whole
1 bay leaf
1 stalk celery
1 tablespoon salt
1½ pounds large, fresh shrimp, shelled and deveined
2 pounds lobster meat, fresh or frozen

1 tablespoon lemon juice
½ teaspoon ginger
½ teaspoon coriander
½ teaspoon cardamon
¼ teaspoon cayenne
½ teaspoon turmeric
1 teaspoon sweet paprika
1 teaspoon salt
¼ teaspoon white pepper

1. Bring water to a boil with garlic, bay leaf, celery, and salt. Add shrimp and cook for 3 to 5 minutes, or until they are just pink. Remove the shrimp immediately and run under cold water.
2. Grind shrimp and lobster, together with lemon juice, 3 times. Place in a large bowl.
3. Add the remaining seasonings and blend well.
4. Stuff into casings, tying off at 4- to 6-inch intervals.
5. Fry very gently in butter until lightly browned and cooked through.

Spanish sausage   *(Yields about 3 pounds)*

Quite different from the standard chorizo, although interchangeable in many recipes.

1½ pounds lean pork
1½ pounds pork fat
3 tablespoons salt
¾ teaspoon cayenne
¼ teaspoon nutmeg
¼ teaspoon ground ginger

¾ teaspoon freshly ground black pepper
1 teaspoon sugar
3 garlic cloves, crushed
½ cup raisins

1. Cube the pork and fat, mix together, and grind coarsely.
2. Add salt, cayenne, nutmeg, ginger, black pepper, and sugar and mix well. Add the garlic and raisins and thoroughly blend, using your hands.
3. Stuff meat carefully into casings and tie off in 4- to 5-inch links. Smoke overnight. This sausage is delicious sliced cold or cooked in soup.

NOTE: As a variation, follow steps 1 and 2 and then continue as follows: Heat ¼ cup olive oil in a large, heavy skillet and sauté the meat mixture until thoroughly cooked. Serve with a tomato sauce or over plain or saffron rice.

Extended and Meatless Sausage Recipes

The popularity of gruetzwurst, which has oatmeal in it, or Scandinavian potatiskorv, made with potatoes, is proof enough that many people prefer sausages made with ingredients other than all meat.

The practice of extending sausages began as an economy measure, and it is still a good way of making your meat dollars go farther. Many commercial and some homemade sausages are extended with fat. But additional fats in your diet serve no positive nutritional purpose and should be avoided. Soy beans or natural grains will do the same job and be an excellent source of protein as well. The most common ingredients used as extenders are soy beans, oats, barley, hominy, and potatoes—Jewish kishkes are made without any meat at all.

As a general rule, you can substitute extenders for up to one half of the meat requirement. We have found that using any more than that makes the flavor and/or texture deteriorate. For best results, use between one fourth and one half of the total meat requirement. Soy beans are our favorite extender.

Also included in this section are recipes for dishes like head cheese, scrapple, and haggis. Although they do not fulfill the dictionary definition for sausages, they do use tag ends of meat, and are generally considered along with sausages in any cookbook.

Gruetzwurst   *(Yields about 10 pounds)*

This sausage is traditionally extended with oatmeal, but you can also try it with soy beans.

5 pounds lean pork
1½ pounds lean beef
3 tablespoons butter or margarine
4 medium onions, finely chopped
3¾ cups cooked oatmeal

1¼ tablespoons sage
½ teaspoon allspice
½ teaspoon summer savory
1 tablespoon salt
½ teaspoon freshly ground black pepper

1. Place the pork and beef in a large pot with water to cover. Bring to a boil, cover, reduce heat, and simmer until very tender. Drain and cool.
2. Cube the meats, mix together, and grind.
3. Melt the butter and sauté the onions until soft, but not browned.
4. Add the onions and oatmeal to the meat mixture and mix well.
5. Add the sage, allspice, savory, salt, and pepper, and mix until thoroughly blended.
6. Stuff into casings, tying off at 4- to 5-inch intervals.
7. Place sausages in a large pot with water to cover. Bring to a boil, cover, reduce heat, and simmer for 45 minutes. Drain.
8. Store what you will use quickly in the refrigerator and freeze the rest.
9. You can eat gruetzwurst cold, or reheated in water, but avoid frying—they're not as good.

Haggis   *(Yields 1 large sausage)*

A Scottish feast attraction, traditionally served at Hogmanay, the New Year's Eve celebration, or at Burns Night, a feast that commemorates the poet Robert Burns.

1 sheep's stomach ⎫
1 sheep's heart   ⎬ will probably need
1 sheep's liver   ⎪ to be ordered in
1 pair sheep's lungs ⎭ advance from
your butcher.
3 large onions, peeled
2 cups Scotch oatmeal

1 cup beef suet, trimmed and minced
2 tablespoons chopped parsley
salt and pepper
whiskey

1. Wash and scrape the stomach well, inside and out, rinsing thoroughly several times. Place in a large bowl, cover with well-salted water, and allow to soak overnight in refrigerator.

2. Wash the heart, liver, and lungs well, rinsing several times. Trim carefully, cutting away windpipe and tendons.

3. Place the heart, liver, and lung in a heavy pot. Sprinkle evenly with 2 teaspoons salt and cover completely with boiling water. Simmer over medium-high heat for 2 hours. Drain, reserving stock; set aside to cool.

4. Trim heart, liver, and lungs of any stringy pieces. Mince very finely heart and lungs and half of the liver. Discard remaining liver.

5. In a small saucepan, boil the onions in salted water to cover for 15 minutes. Cool and chop finely.

6. Spread the oatmeal in an even layer in a jelly-roll pan and toast in a 350° F oven for 20 minutes.

7. Combine the meat, onions, oatmeal, suet, parsley, 1 tablespoon salt, ½ teaspoon pepper and 2½ cups of reserved stock. Fill stomach about half full; sew securely closed.

8. Fill a large pot or kettle with salted water and bring to a boil. Lower haggis carefully into the water and simmer just below the boiling point for 3 hours. Prick occasionally with a needle.

9. Remove haggis from pot carefully and allow to drain briefly in a strainer. Place on a serving platter.

10. Slice at table and serve hot with whiskey. Guests may sprinkle the whiskey over the haggis as liberally as they choose. Although haggis is the main attraction of the New Year's Eve and Burns Night feasts, it is generally served as an accompaniment to other meats.

Head cheese   *(Serves 8 to 12)*

Neither sausage nor cheese, but rather a jellied meat mixture. We'll give the recipe "from scratch," but if you don't have a calf's or hog's head, substitute 3 to 4 pounds of meat for the head and cut the seasonings by about half.

1 calf's or hog's head
2 medium onions, studded with 10 cloves
4 carrots, scraped and halved
6 peppercorns
1 bay leaf
4 stalks of celery
1½ pounds cooked chicken

1½ pounds cooked ham
12 cups beef or chicken stock
6 tablespoons unflavored gelatin
4 tablespoons lemon juice
4 tablespoons white wine
1 tablespoon salt
freshly ground black pepper

1. Quarter the head. Remove eyes, ears, brains, snout, and as much fat as possible. If desired, reserve brains for vinaigrette sauce (see step 12). Clean teeth with a very stiff brush.

2. Soak the pieces for 5 to 6 hours to remove blood, changing the water 2 or 3 times.

3. Wash the pieces well and place in a large pot or kettle with water to cover. Add onions studded with cloves, carrots, peppercorns, bay leaf, and celery. Simmer for about 1½ hours or until meat begins to fall from the bones.

4. Add the chicken and ham and cook for 1 hour more.

5. Remove meats and let cool, allowing the stock to continue simmering.

6. Cube half of the meat into ½-inch pieces and coarsely chop the rest.

7. Place the cubed and chopped meats in alternating layers in molds or loaf pans.

8. Place hot stock in a large bowl. Add the gelatin, lemon juice, and wine, and stir until the gelatin is dissolved. Add the salt.

9. Ladle stock over the meat until completely covered and grind fresh pepper over the top of each mold or loaf.

10. Chill in refrigerator for about 2 hours. Then cover with a cloth and weight down the top (bricks are good for this).

11. Refrigerate at least overnight before serving.

12. To serve, slice and serve with vinaigrette sauce made with 3 parts oil to 1 part vinegar and seasoned with salt, pepper, and a small bit of garlic, if desired. You may add the diced and cooked brains to the sauce, if you wish.

Kishke   *(Serves 4 to 6)*

This is a popular dish in the Kosher delicatessens of New York City; try roasting it along with a chicken and serving it with the chicken gravy as an alternative to dressing. Serve kishke as a rare treat—you wouldn't want to eat this much chicken fat too often!

2 cups sifted flour
½ cup matzo meal
2½ teaspoons salt
1 teaspoon freshly ground black pepper
2 teaspoons sweet paprika

1 large onion, grated
1¼ cups rendered chicken fat
1 18-inch piece of beef casing
2 large onions, sliced
½ teaspoon caraway seeds

1. Blend together the flour, matzo meal, salt, pepper, paprika, grated onion, and 1 cup of the chicken fat.
2. Knot one end of the casing and stuff loosely with the mixture; knot open end securely.
3. Place the kishke in a pot with salted water to cover. Bring to a boil over high heat. Lower heat to medium and simmer for ½ hour.
4. Preheat oven to 350° F. Spread ¼ cup of chicken fat in the bottom of a roasting pan and sprinkle with half of the sliced onions. Center the kishke on top of this; sprinkle with the remaining sliced onions and caraway seeds.
5. Roast kishke in the center of the oven for 1½ hours, basting often. Slice and serve alone or as a side dish.

95

Meat-oatmeal sausage   *(Yields about 4½ pounds)*

This is a good basic sausage that can be a part of breakfast, lunch, or dinner. Vary the spices to create many different flavors.

2½ pounds pork tenderloin	½ teaspoon mace
¾ pound veal	½ teaspoon allspice
1 pound pork fat	⅛ teaspoon ginger
2¼ cups cooked rolled oats	1½ tablespoons salt
1 tablespoon caraway seeds	¼ teaspoon white pepper

1. Cube the meats and fat, mix together, and grind.
2. Add the remaining ingredients and thoroughly blend, using your hands.
3. Stuff into casings, tying off at desired intervals. Store in refrigerator and use within 3 to 4 days.
4. To cook, boil for a few minutes in water to cover, then fry until browned.

Pork-soy bean sausage   *(Yields about 6 pounds)*

2 cups dried soy beans	½ teaspoon ginger
1½ cups water	½ teaspoon allspice
2½ pounds lean pork	1½ tablespoons salt
1 pound smoked pork butt	¼ teaspoon pepper
2 pounds pork fat	

1. Place soy beans in water. Cover, bring to a boil, and boil for 8 to 10 minutes. Drain.
2. Chop the soy beans into very small—no more than ⅛ inch—pieces, or grind. Cool.
3. Cube the meats and fat, mix together, and grind.
4. Add the beans, spices, salt, and pepper and mix well.
5. Knead the mixture for 5 minutes.
6. Stuff into casings, tying off at 5-inch intervals, larger or smaller, if desired. Store in refrigerator and use within 3 to 4 days.
7. To cook, boil or fry.

Potatiskorv   *(Yields 3½ pounds)*

A Swedish potato sausage. This sounds like plain fare, but wait until you bite into it!

2 pounds lean beef
    or
1 pound lean beef plus 1 pound lean veal
4-6 medium potatoes (1½ pounds), peeled and diced
3 medium onions, finely chopped

½ cup cold water
2½ tablespoons salt
1 teaspoon white pepper
1 teaspoon sugar
½ teaspoon freshly ground black pepper
2½ teaspoons allspice

1. Cube the meat. Mix with potatoes and onions and grind coarsely.
2. Add water, salt, white pepper, sugar, black pepper, and allspice. Mix thoroughly, using your hands.
3. Stuff into casings, tying off into small links, about 2 to 2½ inches long.
4. Put sausages into a heavy pot or kettle and cover with boiling water. Cover pot and simmer gently for 1 hour. Drain and serve.

Scandinavian Christmas sausage   *(Yields 5 pounds)*

Sausage:
- 3½ pounds lean pork
- ¾ pound fatback
- 1½ tablespoons salt
- 1¼ teaspoons allspice
- 1 teaspoon ginger
- 2-4 (½ pound) medium potatoes, boiled and mashed, or ⅓ cup cornstarch
- ¾ cup beef stock

Curing Mix:
- 4½ tablespoons salt
- 2½ tablespoons sugar

Brine:
- 1 quart water
- ⅓ cup coarse (Kosher) salt
- 1 tablespoon sugar

1. Cube the pork and fatback, mix together, and grind finely.
2. Add salt, allspice, ginger, potatoes or cornstarch, and beef stock. The mixture should hold together. To check, drop about a tablespoon of the mixture into rapidly boiling water. If it doesn't hold together, add more potatoes.
3. Stuff into casings loosely and tie off at 12-inch intervals, cutting each link off as you go, instead of leaving them in chains.
4. Rinse each link with cold water and dry thoroughly.
5. Combine the curing ingredients and rub the sausages all over with the mixture.
6. Refrigerate overnight.
7. If you want to keep the sausages for more than a few days, you will either have to freeze them or keep them in brine. To make the brine, combine the ingredients and boil for about 5 minutes. Let cool and add the sausages. Serve at room temperature.

Scrapple   *(Serves 10)*

Not officially a sausage, but since it's made from minced meats, scrapple is usually classed along with sausages. Another name for it is "ponhaws," and if you substitute rolled oats for the cornmeal, you've got "goetta."

3½ pounds pork neck	2 teaspoons finely chopped onion
½ pound pork liver	1 teaspoon thyme
2 medium onions	1 teaspoon marjoram
1 bay leaf	½ teaspoon sage
10 to 12 whole peppercorns	½ teaspoon cayenne
2 cups cornmeal	½ teaspoon nutmeg
1 tablespoon salt	¼ teaspoon cloves

1. Place neck, liver, 2 onions, bay leaf, and peppercorns in a large pot with water to cover. Bring to a boil, cover, reduce heat, and simmer for 1 hour, or until meat begins to fall from bones. Drain, reserving 3 cups of the stock. Remove meat from bones and mince with the liver.

2. Place cornmeal and salt in a large, heavy saucepan. Stir in the reserved stock and cook slowly over medium heat, stirring constantly, until the liquid is absorbed and the cornmeal becomes very thick.

3. Add the meats, chopped onion, spices, and salt, and mix well. Cover and cook over low heat for 1 hour, stirring occasionally.

4. Pour mixture into a bread pan. Let stand at room temperature until cooled and firm. Refrigerate and use within 3 to 4 days.

5. To cook, slice and sauté in butter or margarine until well browned on both sides.

6. Serve with honey, maple syrup, molasses, or cinnamon sugar.

Tel Aviv "hot dogs"   *(Yields about 20)*

In Israel these are sold by vendors on street corners, served in pita bread with a tahini dressing. They may also be known as falafel.

1 pound dried chickpeas (garbanzo beans)
1 cup soft bread crumbs
2 eggs, slightly beaten
3 cloves garlic, crushed
1 teaspoon salt
½ teaspoon pepper
2 teaspoons cumin seed
1 teaspoon cayenne
½ teaspoon oregano
¼ teaspoon dried hot red pepper flakes
½ teaspoon baking powder
olive oil

1. Rinse the chickpeas well and soak for 8 hours, or overnight, in salted water to cover. Drain.
2. In a large bowl, mix the chickpeas with the bread crumbs and grind together.
3. Combine the ground chickpeas with the eggs and garlic and blend well. Add the remaining spices and baking powder and mix again.
4. Form the mixture into sausage shapes about 4 inches long and about ¾ inch thick. Chill for at least 1 hour.
5. Deep fry in very hot oil until well browned. The sausages should puff slightly and be light and crisp.

Cooking With Sausage

Now that you've learned how to make a few dozen different kinds of sausage, we'd like to show you how versatile they can be. Here are recipes that use sausages as appetizers, in soups and breads, as main dishes for breakfast, lunch, and dinner—there are even two dessert sausages, one that we've developed and are particularly proud of.

All the following recipes use sausages that are detailed in the preceding sections. Whenever pertinent, we give you a choice of sausages or suggest possible substitutions. Feel free to adapt and substitute—before you know it you might create a family classic!

APPETIZERS

Babi's sulc   (*Serves 12*)

Babi was our grandmother, and this head cheese was her New Year's Eve specialty.

4 pig's knuckles
2 pig's feet
1 cup diced onions
2 cloves garlic, minced

1 bay leaf, crumbled
1 tablespoon whole peppercorns
1 cup white vinegar
salt to taste

1. Clean knuckles and feet very well. Place in a large, heavy pot with water to cover.
2. Add onions, garlic, bay leaf, peppercorns, salt, and ½ cup white vinegar, and bring to a boil over high heat. Lower heat to medium and cook, uncovered, until the meat is just about falling off the bones. Remove from heat.
3. Trim fat and skin from meat. Cut meat into small pieces. Scrape fat from skin and cut skin into thin strips about 1½ inches long. Discard fat. Set meat and skin aside.
4. Strain stock and bring to a boil. Add the meat, skin, and remaining vinegar and bring to a boil again.
5. Pour the mixture into loaf pans or decorative molds and allow to cool at room temperature. Cover and refrigerate until set completely.
6. Unmold. Slice and serve with additional vinegar.

Cocktail wieners   *(Yields 2 dozen)*

2 tablespoons Dijon mustard	¼ teaspoon allspice
2 tablespoons tomato catsup	¼ teaspoon cloves
2½ teaspoons onion juice	2 dozen cocktail-size frankfurters
½ teaspoon tarragon	

1. In a saucepan, mix together all ingredients except sausages.
2. Bring to a boil, add sausages, and simmer over low heat for about 15 minutes.
3. Turn into a chafing dish for serving.

Edy Orr's sylta (Serves about 40)

This version of head cheese comes from a Swedish friend.

2 pig's feet
3 pounds very fatty shoulder of pork
3 pounds breast or shoulder of veal
5 or 6 bay leaves
12 whole allspice

10 whole white peppercorns in a small cloth bag
2 large onions, sliced
2 cups celery, cut in 1-inch slices
2 carrots, sliced
large pieces of pig skin

1. Wash pork and veal. Place in a large pot with water to cover and bring to a boil over high heat.
2. Add the remaining ingredients except pig skin and lower heat to medium. Simmer until meats are soft and tender. Remove meats and set aside. Strain, and reserve liquid.
3. Soak a large, clean dish towel in cold water. Wring out, and spread carefully inside a large, round mold; let edges of towel drape over sides. (Edy uses a large cast iron frying pan for her mold.)
4. On top of the towel, line the mold completely with the pig skin, being sure to save enough to top the filled mold.
5. Slice the pork and veal and set aside. Remove fat and skin from pig's feet. Slice the skin and meat and discard the fat.
6. Place alternate layers of the sliced meats in the lined mold, seasoning each layer well with salt and pepper. Top the meats with a layer of pork skin. Gather the edges of the towel together tightly and tie securely.
7. Bring the reserved liquid to a boil in a large pot. Place the towel-wrapped sylta in the

hot liquid, lower heat to medium-high, and boil 30 minutes. Drain, and discard liquid.

8. Place sylta on a platter and weight with a heavy cutting board, or any flat, heavy object, and leave overnight at room temperature.

9. At this point, Edy puts her sylta in the cellar for about 48 hours or until it sets and then refrigerates it until she is ready to use it. It will keep in the refrigerator up to 1 week. Unwrap and slice to serve.

Fried sausage canapes   *(Yields 36)*

 9 slices day-old white bread
½ pound basic bulk sausage
 2 eggs, beaten lightly
¼ cup minced parsley

½ teaspoon freshly ground black
    pepper
 2 tablespoons tomato paste
vegetable oil

1. Remove crusts from the bread and, using a cookie cutter, cut 36 circles—4 from each slice. Since loaf sizes vary, you may need 1 or 2 extra slices of bread to make the 36 circles.

2. In a large bowl, combine the sausage meat with the eggs, parsley, pepper, and tomato paste. Blend thoroughly, using your hands.

3. Spread each round of bread with a generous mound of the mixture.

4. Heat 2 inches of oil in a heavy skillet over medium heat.

5. When the oil is very hot, drop bread rounds in carefully, sausage side up, and fry 3 to 4 minutes; turn and fry 3 to 4 minutes longer. Drain and serve hot.

105

NOTE: These can be made even more attractive by using cookie cutters in fancy shapes, but don't use anything too complicated or too large.

Marinated kielbasa   *(Serves 10)*

1 large (3- to 4-pound) kielbasa
8 scallions, finely chopped
1 tomato, finely chopped
6 tablespoons minced parsley
½ cup white vinegar
½ teaspoon sugar

1 teaspoon salt
½ teaspoon freshly ground black
    pepper
¼ cup vegetable oil
½ teaspoon Dijon mustard

1. Slice kielbasa into ½-inch rounds.
2. Place in a bowl with scallions, tomato, and parsley.
3. Mix together vinegar, sugar, salt, pepper, oil, and mustard, and pour over ingredients in bowl.
4. Toss lightly and refrigerate for several hours or overnight.
5. Serve with rounds of rye or pumpernickel bread and a tray of fresh vegetables, such as radishes, celery, carrots, and scallions.

Pickled knackwurst   *(Serves 6)*

This will keep in your refrigerator for several weeks.

5½ cups water
3½ cups white vinegar
¼ cup sugar
about 30 whole allspice
1 tablespoon black peppercorns

3½ teaspoons salt
1 tablespoon caraway seeds
2 large Bermuda onions
3 pounds knackwurst

1. In a heavy pot or kettle, combine the water, vinegar, sugar, allspice, peppercorns, salt, and caraway seeds. Cover and bring to a boil over high heat; reduce heat to medium and simmer for 15 minutes. Set aside.

2. Peel the onions and slice as thinly as possible, separating into rings. Slice the knackwurst into ½-inch rounds.

3. In a gallon jar or crock (or even a large bowl), build alternate layers of knackwurst and onion rings, beginning with the knackwurst.

4. Pour marinade over all. Cover and refrigerate for 3 or 4 days before using. This gets better the longer it marinates. To vary the visual appeal a little, try using red onions instead of Bermuda onions.

Potted liverwurst   *(Yields about 1½ pounds)*

Very good with cocktails, this can also be a deliciously decadent lunch with thin slices of good, dark bread.

1 pound liverwurst, uncased	⅓ cup chopped parsley
½ pint sour cream	½ teaspoon thyme
¾ pound fresh mushrooms, minced	½ teaspoon sage
½ cup clarified butter, melted	½ teaspoon freshly ground black pepper
	⅓ cup cognac or brandy

107

1. Allow sausage and sour cream to reach room temperature. Blend together well, using a wooden spoon.

2. In a heavy skillet, sauté the mushrooms in ¼ cup of the clarified butter until well browned. Add the parsley, thyme, sage, and black pepper, and sauté for 2 minutes more.

3. Combine with the sausage. Add the cognac a little at a time, mashing continuously with a wooden spoon until soft and smooth.

4. Pack sausage mixture tightly into small bowls, cups, or crocks; top with a thin layer of the remaining clarified butter. Refrigerate overnight and use within one week.

Samosas   *(Yields about 3 dozen)*

Samosas are Indian curried meat turnovers, which we have adapted for use with sausage meat.

Filling:
2 tablespoons butter
2 tablespoons minced onion
1 clove garlic, minced
½ teaspoon cinnamon
¼ teaspoon ginger
1 teaspoon coriander
1 pound basic bulk sausage, using pork/beef combination and omitting thyme, basil, and sage.
¼ cup water
2 teaspoons fresh lemon juice
¼ cup seedless raisins
1 teaspoon salt

Pastry:
2 cups sifted all-purpose flour
¼ teaspoon white pepper
1 teaspoon salt
¼ cup melted butter
½ cup + 1 tablespoon plain yogurt

2 egg whites, beaten lightly with 1 teaspoon water
fat for deep frying

1. Melt butter in a heavy skillet. Add onion and garlic and sauté 3 minutes. Add cinnamon, ginger, and coriander, and continue to sauté, stirring, for 1 minute more.

2. Add sausage meat to skillet and sauté, stirring, until meat begins to lose its red color. Blend in water and lemon juice and cook until liquid is absorbed, stirring occasionally.

3. Add raisins and salt and toss to mix evenly. Spread meat on a platter to cool.

4. Meanwhile, prepare pastry: Sift together the flour, white pepper, and salt. Add the butter all at once and mix with a fork.

5. Add the yogurt, a little at a time, using your hands to blend evenly.

6. Knead the dough on a floured surface until smooth and satiny.

7. Using half of the pastry at a time for convenience in handling, roll very thin on a well-floured board or pastry cloth. Using a round cookie cutter or the rim of a drinking glass, cut 2½-inch circles from the pastry. Place a small mound of filling on each circle and, using a pastry brush, moisten the edges with egg white. Fold circles over in half and crimp edges with a fork dipped in cold water. Be sure to seal tightly. Set samosas aside on waxed paper as they are ready.

8. Fry samosas in hot fat until crisp and golden in color. Drain and serve hot.

Sausage paté *(Yields 1½ pounds)*

¼ cup pine nuts
1¾ pounds basic bulk sausage, using 2 parts pork to 1 part veal, ground twice
⅓ cup soft, oil-cured black olives
¼ cup diced prosciutto
¼ cup soft bread crumbs

1½ teaspoons chopped fresh basil
1 tablespoon chopped parsley
3 tablespoons dry vermouth
1 clove garlic, crushed
1 egg, lightly beaten
fatback, cut in strips

109

1. Spread pine nuts on a cookie sheet and roast at 250° F for 20 minutes.
2. Combine sausage, nuts, olives, prosciutto, bread crumbs, basil, and parsley. Mash together with a wooden spoon while moistening with the vermouth.
3. Add the garlic and beaten egg and blend well.
4. Line the bottom of a loaf pan with strips of fatback. Press the sausage mixture firmly into the loaf pan and lay strips of fatback across the top to cover.
5. Bake at 350° F for 1½ hours. Remove from oven, weight the paté with a heavy cutting board, or any flat, heavy object, and cool at room temperature.
6. Refrigerate for 12 hours. Unmold and remove fatback. Allow to reach room temperature before serving.

Sausage-pistachio biscuit roll   (*Serves 12*)

Biscuit dough:
2 cups all-purpose flour
2½ teaspoons baking powder
½ teaspoon salt
¼ teaspoon sugar
5 tablespoons butter, as cold as possible, and cut in small pieces
⅔ cup cold milk, approximately

Filling:
¼ cup butter
¼ cup minced onion
2 cloves garlic, minced
1 pound basic bulk sausage, uncased
½ cup skinned pistachio nuts
2 tablespoons minced parsley

1. For crust, sift together the flour, baking powder, salt, and sugar.
2. Using a pastry blender, cut butter into dry ingredients until the mixture resembles coarse meal.
3. Add milk a little at a time, stirring with a fork, to make a soft dough.

4. Turn dough onto a floured board or pastry cloth. Knead for 1 minute, dust with flour, and wrap in waxed paper or plastic wrap. Chill.

5. For filling, melt ¼ cup butter in a heavy skillet. Add onion and garlic and sauté until onion is soft.

6. Remove skillet from heat and stir in sausage meat. Sauté, stirring, until meat loses its red color. Stir in pistachio nuts and parsley. Place mixture in a large bowl and set aside.

7. On a floured surface, roll half of the dough into a large rectangle about ⅛ inch thick. Spread with half of the sausage mixture and roll like a jelly roll. Repeat with remaining dough and filling. Chill both rolls for 10 minutes.

8. Slice the rolls ½ inch thick. Lay slices flat on cookie sheets and bake at 425° F for 10 minutes. Turn slices and bake for 10 minutes more. Serve hot.

Scotch eggs   *(Serves 6)*

7 large eggs	milk or water
1¼ pounds breakfast, Midwest farmhouse, or Missouri pork sausage	flour
	bread crumbs
	oil for deep frying

1. Hard cook 6 of the eggs. Plunge in cold water and peel.
2. Enclose each egg with a generous coating of sausage meat.
3. Beat the remaining egg with a small amount of milk or water.
4. Bread each egg by first dusting with flour, then dipping in beaten egg, and finally coating with bread crumbs.
5. Deep fry in very hot fat until the sausage meat is well browned and cooked through.
6. Drain well and serve garnished with parsley.

Toasted sausage and horseradish canapes   *(Yields 24)*

12 slices two-day-old white bread
½ cup soft butter
¾ pound kielbasa, skinned and
   chopped

6 tablespoons sour cream
½ cup grated fresh horseradish
1½ teaspoons flour
1½ tablespoons sour cream

1. Spread butter on both sides of each slice of bread.
2. Cut each piece in half.
3. Mix the sausage with the 6 tablespoons sour cream and spread on each piece of bread.
4. Mix the horseradish with the flour and sour cream and spread over the sausage.
5. Bake at 450° F for 10 minutes.

SOUPS

Beef soup with liver dumplings   *(Serves 4 to 6)*

Soup:
2 stalks celery, diced
2 medium carrots, diced
1 potato, diced
1 medium onion, diced
2 tablespoons oil
6 cups beef consommé
1½ tablespoons chervil
1½ tablespoons chopped parsley

Dumplings:
¾ pound liverwurst, uncased
1 egg
1 cup bread crumbs
1 tablespoon chopped parsley
1 tablespoon chopped chives
2 tablespoons tomato catsup

112

1. To make soup, sauté celery, carrots, potatoes, and onion in oil until soft but not browned. Add 2 cups consommé and cook until vegetables are tender.
2. To prepare dumplings, mix all the dumpling ingredients together and roll with your hands into 1½-inch dumplings.
3. Add the remaining consommé to pot with vegetables and heat through.
4. Drop dumplings into soup and simmer for 5 minutes or until heated through.
5. Add chervil and parsley to soup, stir, and serve.

Cabbage soup with knackwurst   *(Serves 8)*

This is Scandinavian in origin. You can substitute kielbasa or frankfurters for the knackwurst.

2 large heads cabbage, shredded	freshly ground pepper to taste
¼ pound butter or margarine	1 teaspoon allspice
2½ tablespoons brown sugar	2 quarts chicken stock
1 tablespoon salt	4 knackwursts, sliced 1 inch thick

1. In a large kettle or pot, sauté cabbage in butter over low heat until nicely browned.
2. Add sugar, salt, pepper, and allspice and simmer, covered, for 25 minutes. Stir frequently to prevent sticking.
3. Add stock, cover, and let simmer ½ hour more, or until cabbage is very tender.
4. Add knackwurst and cook 15 minutes more, or until a knackwurst is cooked through.
5. Pour into bowls and garnish with parsley.

Caldo verde   *(Serves 6)*

Many sausages lend themselves beautifully to soups, and chorizo is no exception.

4 large potatoes, boiled and peeled
2 tablespoons milk
2 cloves garlic, crushed
1½ quarts water

1½ tablespoons olive oil
6 cups savoy cabbage, shredded
1½ pounds chorizo, cut into ½-inch slices
salt and pepper to taste

1. Mash the potatoes with the milk until soft and fluffy. Add the garlic and blend well.
2. Bring the water to a boil in a large pot or kettle. Slowly add the potatoes and oil to the boiling water, stirring constantly with a large whisk. Continue stirring until slightly thickened, then add the cabbage.
3. Simmer for 1 hour, stirring occasionally, until the cabbage is tender.
4. Divide the sausages evenly among 6 soup bowls. Pour the soup over the sausages, add salt and pepper, and serve hot with bread.

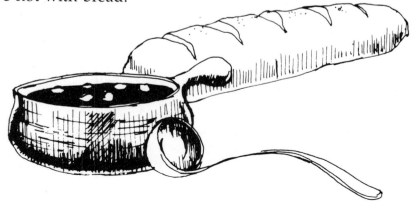

Garbure   (Serves 6 to 8)

This thick soup is called garbure *in southern France,* potée *in the north.*

1 medium head of cabbage, cut in wedges
1 pound bacon, in one piece
¼ pound pork rind
8 carrots, peeled and cut in half lengthwise
8 tiny onions
3 leeks, sliced
6 medium potatoes, peeled and cut in half
1 cup fresh or frozen peas

½ pound green beans, trimmed, washed, and cut in half
¼ cup butter
½ pound French garlic sausages
½ pound Midwest farmhouse or Missouri pork sausages
½ cup red wine (optional)
crusty bread
freshly ground black pepper to taste

1. Blanch the cabbage wedges in boiling water for 10 minutes. Drain and shred.
2. Place the bacon and pork rind in a large, heavy pot or kettle with water to cover, and bring to a boil over high heat. Lower heat to medium and simmer for ½ hour.
3. Add the carrots, onions, leeks, potatoes, peas, and green beans and simmer for ½ hour more.
4. Meanwhile, melt the butter in a heavy skillet and brown the sausages for 10 minutes. Drain and slice.
5. Remove bacon and rind from pot, slice, and return to pot with cabbage and sausages. Add wine, if desired. Simmer for 10 minutes.
6. Place a thick slice of bread in the bottom of each soup bowl, and ladle soup over bread. Grind pepper directly into bowl and enjoy.

115

Gulyasleves   *(Serves 6)*

This is an old Hungarian recipe for a "goulash soup." It is a meal in itself.

½ pound knackwurst
¼ cup butter
2½ cups chopped onions
1 cup chopped green pepper
¾ pound lean pork, cut into
    1-inch cubes
¾ pound beef, cut into 1-inch
    cubes
1 cup coarsely chopped ripe
    tomatoes

1 teaspoon salt
1 teaspoon freshly ground black
    pepper
2 tablespoons sweet paprika
½ teaspoon cayenne
½ teaspoon garlic powder
1 quart + 1 cup boiling water
1½ cups thickly sliced potatoes

1. Place the knackwurst in a pot with water to cover. Bring to a boil, lower heat, and simmer for 15 minutes. Drain, cut in chunks, and set aside.

2. Melt the butter in a heavy pot or kettle. Add the onions and green pepper and sauté, stirring, for 10 minutes. Add the pork and beef and cook over medium heat until well browned.

3. Add the tomatoes, salt, pepper, paprika, cayenne, garlic powder, and boiling water. Bring to a boil. Cover pot tightly, lower heat, and simmer for 1½ hours.

4. Add the potato slices and stir carefully. Cover again and continue cooking for ½ hour. Add the knackwurst and cook 10 minutes more. Serve hot.

116

Pot au feu with kielbasa   (*Serves 8*)

Our own adaptation of a traditional French dish.

1 4- to 5-pound beef brisket (or use beef short ribs)
1 whole cabbage, cored
3 medium onions, quartered
4 cloves garlic, whole
3 carrots, peeled and quartered
4 leeks, chopped
1 bay leaf
12 whole black peppercorns
1 tablespoon rosemary
1 teaspoon thyme
1 teaspoon tarragon
1 tablespoon chopped parsley
8 cloves
salt

1 chicken, cut in serving pieces
10 to 15 small new potatoes, washed, with skins left on
2 large kielbasa
3 tablespoons olive oil
1 large onion, diced
2 6-ounce cans tomato paste
1 teaspoon thyme
salt and pepper
grated fresh horseradish
cornichons (small French pickles)
Dijon mustard
Kosher (coarse) salt
freshly ground black pepper

1. Place brisket and cabbage, with water to cover, in a pot large enough to accommodate all of the remaining ingredients. Bring to a boil, reduce heat, cover, and simmer for about 20 minutes.
2. Add the quartered onions, garlic, carrots, leeks, bay leaf, peppercorns, rosemary, thyme, tarragon, parsley, cloves, and salt to taste. Cover and simmer for 45 minutes more.
3. Add chicken, potatoes, and kielbasa, cover, and continue simmering for 1 hour more.

117

4. Meanwhile, prepare a tomato sauce. Heat the olive oil and add the onion. Sauté until golden. Add the tomato paste, thyme, 2 tomato-paste cans of the stock, and salt and pepper to taste. Simmer, uncovered, for about 15 minutes.

5. Slice the brisket and sausages and arrange on a platter with the vegetables.

6. Serve tomato sauce, horseradish, cornichons, Dijon mustard, Kosher salt, and pepper as accompaniments.

BREADS, STUFFINGS, AND PIZZAS

Cornbread with sausage   *(Yields 1 8-by-12-inch bread)*

1½ pounds breakfast sausage links
1 can cranberry sauce (whole berries, not jellied)
1 cup flour
1½ teaspoons salt
⅓ cup sugar

1 cup wheat germ
1 cup cornmeal
1¼ cups milk
4 large eggs
⅓ cup melted butter or margarine

1. Preheat oven to 400° F. Grease an 8-by-12-inch shallow pan.
2. Fry the sausages until well browned and cooked through. Arrange in a single layer in the pan.
3. Spoon the cranberry sauce over the sausages and set aside.
4. In a bowl, combine the flour, salt, sugar, wheat germ, and cornmeal. Blend well.
5. Pour the milk into a separate bowl. Beat in the eggs and melted butter.

6. Stir the milk mixture into the dry ingredients until moistened. The batter will be lumpy.
7. Spoon batter over the cranberry sauce.
8. Bake for 30 minutes, or until done.

Ingrid's sausage stuffing   *(Yields enough stuffing for a 15- to 18-pound turkey)*

Our friend, Ingrid Jones, provided us with the recipe for this delicious turkey stuffing.

½ pound breakfast sausage links
turkey giblets
¼ pound butter
¼ cup chopped celery
¼ cup chopped leek

¼ cup chopped onion
¼ cup chopped parsley
1 16-ounce bag seasoned dry stuffing mix, or your own equivalent

1. Put the sausages in a heavy skillet with water to cover. Bring to a boil over high heat. Cover, lower heat to medium, and simmer for 10 minutes. Drain, return skillet to heat, and allow sausages to brown evenly in their own fat. Drain, cut into ½-inch rounds, and set aside.
2. In a saucepan, boil the giblets in 2 cups water for 15 minutes or until they have lost their red color. Drain, reserving the broth. Chop the giblets and set aside.
3. Melt the butter in a large skillet. Add the celery, leek, onion, and parsley, and sauté, stirring, until the vegetables are tender.
4. Add the stuffing mix to the vegetables and stir until blended. Moisten with the reserved broth and mix well. Add the giblets and sausages and mix again. Taste for seasoning, stuff turkey loosely, and roast as usual.

119

Pissaladière *(Makes 1 large "pizza")*

A French "pizza" that we decided to try with sausages.

Crust:
- ½ cup milk
- 1 package dry yeast
- ¼ cup warm water
- ½ cup butter
- ¼ cup + 1 teaspoon sugar
- 3 eggs + 1 egg yolk, beaten
- ½ teaspoon salt
- 3¼ cups sifted all-purpose flour

Topping:
- ½ cup olive oil
- 1 or 2 cloves garlic, minced
- 1½ cups finely chopped onion
- salt and pepper
- 1 6-ounce can tomato paste
- 1 tablespoon minced parsley
- 1 tablespoon minced fresh basil
- ¾ cup sliced Parisian Saucisson
- ¾ cup sliced, dry, black Mediterranean olives

1. To make crust, scald milk; cool to lukewarm.
2. In a small bowl or cup, sprinkle the yeast over the warm water. Wait a few seconds, then stir until dissolved.
3. In a large bowl, cream the butter until it becomes fluffy and light in color. Slowly add sugar and blend well.
4. Add the lukewarm milk and yeast mixture and stir well.
5. Blend in the eggs, salt, and flour. Beat with a wooden spoon for 10 to 12 minutes. Cover and let rise in a warm, draft-free place for 2 hours, or until slightly more than doubled in bulk.
6. Punch down and turn out on a floured board or pastry cloth. Using a floured rolling pin, roll the dough out to ½ inch thick and arrange in an oblong baking pan or on a cookie sheet. Cover and let rise a second time.

7. While crust is rising the second time, heat the oil in a heavy skillet and sauté the garlic and onions for 2 minutes. Lower heat, cover, and simmer until the onions are soft but not browned. Add salt and pepper to taste.

8. Remove the garlic and onions to a bowl, using a slotted spoon to drain slightly. Mix in tomato paste, half of the parsley and half of the basil. Spread on the crust.

9. Arrange sliced sausage and olives decoratively on top of the mixture, and sprinkle with the remaining parsley and basil.

10. Bake at 375° F for 15 to 20 minutes or until the crust is crisp and baked through.

Sausage and fruit stuffing   *(Yields 4 cups)*

2 cups fresh bread crumbs
½ cup milk
2 tablespoons butter
1 small onion, chopped
½ pound basic bulk sausage, uncased
⅓ cup seedless raisins

⅓ cup fresh cranberries, chopped
1 large tart apple, peeled, cored, and diced
1 teaspoon sage
1 teaspoon thyme
¼ cup chopped parsley
salt and pepper to taste

1. Soak bread crumbs in the milk. Squeeze out crumbs and set aside. Discard liquid.

2. Melt the butter in a heavy skillet and sauté the onion until soft. Add the sausage and sauté lightly.

3. Add the fruits and cook, stirring with a wooden spoon, for 5 minutes.

4. Combine the sausage mixture with the bread crumbs in a large bowl. Add sage, thyme, parsley, salt, and pepper, and blend well. This is a particularly good stuffing for a crown roast of pork.

121

Sausage and sweet potato stuffing   *(Yields enough stuffing for a 12- to 15-pound turkey)*

This stuffing has become a Thanksgiving tradition with us. Reduce the quantities and try it with duck, chicken, or goose.

10 medium-sized sweet potatoes
1½ pounds sausage meat, uncased (we recommend Midwest farmhouse or Pennsylvania Dutch)
1 cup chopped onions
1 cup chopped celery
4 cups soft bread crumbs
½ cup raisins

2 tablespoons chopped parsley
¼ teaspoon thyme
¼ teaspoon sage
1½ cups peeled and diced Rome Beauty apples
1½ cups chopped pecans
½ teaspoon nutmeg
½ teaspoon mace
salt and pepper

1. Scrub the sweet potatoes and boil in water to cover until very tender. Peel, mash well, and set aside.
2. Fry the sausage until well done, crumbling with a fork as it cooks. Drain and set aside, reserving pan drippings.
3. Sauté the onions and celery in sausage drippings until the onions are golden brown.
4. In a large bowl, mix together the sweet potatoes, sausage, onions, and celery.
5. Add the bread crumbs, raisins, parsley, thyme, and sage and mix well.
6. Add the apples, pecans, nutmeg, and mace, blending well. Add salt and pepper to taste.
7. Taste stuffing and correct seasonings. Stuff bird loosely and roast as usual.

Sausage muffins I   *(Yields 12 to 15 large muffins)*

A real treat for grownups, and kids love the "surprise" at the bottom.

1 pound breakfast sausage links
4 cups flour
1 teaspoon baking soda
¼ cup cornmeal

1 teaspoon salt
2 large eggs
3 cups buttermilk
3 tablespoons light brown sugar

1. Preheat oven to 400° F. Grease muffin tins.
2. Fry the sausages until well browned and cooked through. Place 1 link in the bottom of each muffin cup.
3. Mix together the flour, baking soda, cornmeal, and salt.
4. Break the eggs into a separate bowl. Beat in the buttermilk and brown sugar.
5. Stir the buttermilk mixture into the dry ingredients until just moistened. The batter will be lumpy.
6. Spoon the batter over the sausages, filling each cup ⅔ full.
7. Bake for 20 minutes, or until done.

Sausage muffins II   *(Yields about 18 muffins)*

9 breakfast sausage links
3 cups sifted all-purpose flour
3 teaspoons baking powder
¾ teaspoon salt

3 tablespoons sugar
1½ cups cold milk
¾ cup melted butter
2 eggs, well beaten

1. Preheat oven to 400° F. Grease muffin tins.
2. Put the sausages in a heavy skillet with water to cover. Bring to a boil. Cover, lower heat to medium, and simmer for 10 minutes. Drain fat from sausages, return skillet to burner, and brown the sausages evenly in their own fat. Drain, cut each link in half, and place 1 piece in the bottom of each muffin cup.
3. Sift the dry ingredients together in a medium-sized bowl.
4. Add the milk and melted butter to the beaten eggs and stir into the dry ingredients until just moistened—leave the batter somewhat lumpy.
5. Spoon the batter over the sausages, filling each cup ⅔ full.
6. Bake for 25 minutes. Serve hot with butter. These are especially good with maple butter.

Sausage pizza   *(Yields two 12-inch pizzas)*

Great for parties or family meals. The dough keeps well in the freezer.

1 package dry yeast
1¼ cups warm water
4 cups flour
½ teaspoon salt
1½ pounds Italian hot, sweet, or fennel sausage, or a combination of all, cased or uncased

2 cups tomato sauce, canned or homemade
2 cups shredded Mozzarella cheese

1. In a large bowl, sprinkle the yeast over water, wait a few seconds, and stir to dissolve. Add flour and salt and beat well.

2. Turn dough onto a floured board and knead for 15 minutes or until dough is smooth and elastic.

3. Oil another bowl and place dough in it. Turn once or twice to make sure the top is oiled. Cover and let rise in a warm place for 30 to 45 minutes or until doubled in bulk.

4. Punch down, turn onto a board, and knead just enough to be certain all large air bubbles have been forced out.

5. Divide dough in half and roll each half out to 11 inches in diameter.

6. Stretch each circle out to fit an oiled 12-inch pizza pan. Set aside.

7. Preheat oven to 450° F.

8. Sauté the sausage in a skillet until well browned. Drain. If you are using cased sausages, cut into ½-inch rounds before frying.

9. Spread 1 cup sauce over each pizza. Spread the sausage meat, or arrange the slices, over sauce.

10. Sprinkle with Mozzarella cheese.

11. Bake for about 25 minutes, changing position in oven halfway through baking.

SIDE DISHES

English sausage custard   *(Serves 6 to 8)*

A good alternative to Yorkshire pudding.

2 pounds basic bulk sausage, uncased
2 tablespoons vegetable oil
1½ cups sifted all-purpose flour
1 clove garlic, minced
1 teaspoon freshly ground black pepper
½ teaspoon salt
1½ cups cold milk
3 eggs, beaten
2 tablespoons minced parsley

1. Form the sausage meat into 1-inch balls. Cover with waxed paper and refrigerate for 1 hour.
2. Preheat oven to 450° F.
3. Heat the oil in a large skillet and fry the sausage balls lightly on all sides. Drain and set aside with ¼ cup of the drippings.
4. Mix the flour, garlic, pepper, and salt in a medium-sized bowl. Add the milk and eggs all at once and mix with an egg beater or electric mixer until smooth. Stir in the parsley.
5. Place the reserved drippings and the sausage balls in a 2-quart casserole or soufflé dish and pour the batter over them.
6. Bake at 450° F for 15 minutes. Lower heat to 350° F and bake 20 minutes more, or until crisp and puffy. If you wish, pass under broiler briefly to crisp further.

Pigs in potatoes   *(Serves 6)*

1 medium onion, minced
1 tablespoon minced parsley
4½ cups mashed potatoes
3 egg yolks
12 tiny (3-inch) precooked pork
   sausages (we recommend
   bratwurst or frankfurters)

cornflake crumbs
2 eggs
3 tablespoons milk
oil for deep frying

1. Beat the onion and parsley into the potatoes. Add the egg yolks and beat well.
2. Coat the sausages with the potato mixture.
3. Roll in cornflake crumbs, then in the eggs beaten with the milk, then in crumbs once more.
4. Deep fry at 375° F until golden brown. Drain and serve.

Potatoes stuffed with sausage   *(Serves 6)*

6 large baking potatoes
salt and pepper
1 pound uncased sausage meat
   (we recommend breakfast sausage or Missouri pork sausage)
2 tablespoons chopped parsley

1 medium onion, chopped
3 tablespoons butter
½ cup beef broth
¼ cup French bread crumbs
¼ cup melted butter

127

1. Preheat oven to 350° F.
2. Peel the potatoes and slice off the ends to make them all the same length.
3. Hollow out a cavity in the end of each potato large enough to hold about 3 table-spoons of stuffing.
4. Drop the potatoes into rapidly boiling salted water and cook for 2 minutes. Remove and pat dry. Place in a buttered, shallow casserole. Sprinkle with salt and pepper to taste. Set aside.
5. Mix the sausage meat with the parsley.
6. Sauté the onions in the butter until golden and mix with the sausage.
7. Stuff the sausage mixture into the cavity of each potato.
8. Bring the broth to a boil and pour over the potatoes so that they are moistened, but not immersed.
9. Cover and bake for 35 minutes.
10. Remove the lid and sprinkle with the bread crumbs and melted butter.
11. Return to oven and bake, uncovered, a few minutes more or until nicely browned.
12. Transfer the potatoes to a serving platter. Boil down the pan juices, strain, and pour over the potatoes.

NOTE: You can also stuff potatoes that have been baked in their skins. Scoop them out and mash with fried sausage meat, parsley, and fried onions, and refill the skins. Sprinkle with bread crumbs and melted butter and bake until browned.

Sausage and sweets   *(Serves 8)*

8 sweet potatoes, cooked
2½ pounds sausage meat shaped
   into 8 flat patties (we recommend Midwest farmhouse or
   Pennsylvania Dutch)
4 strips bacon, fried and crumbled

8 thick slices fresh or canned
   pineapple
salt
cinnamon sugar
milk

1. Preheat oven to 350° F.
2. Peel the sweet potatoes and cut into ¼-inch slices. Place half the slices in the bottom of a greased baking pan.
3. Lightly brown the sausage patties on both sides. Add the bacon and brown a few minutes more. Drain.
4. Lay the cooked patties on top of the sweet potato slices.
5. Cover with the pineapple slices and sprinkle with salt and cinnamon sugar.
6. Cover with the remaining sweet potato slices.
7. Brush milk over the potatoes and sprinkle with cinnamon sugar.
8. Bake for 45 minutes to 1 hour.

Sausage-stuffed tomatoes   (Serves 8)

8 firm, ripe tomatoes
salt
olive oil
1¼ cups minced onion
2 cloves garlic, crushed
1 pound basic bulk sausage
1 teaspoon oregano

1 teaspoon basil
1 teaspoon chopped parsley
¼ cup grated Romano cheese
1¾ cups bread crumbs
½ cup milk
2 egg yolks, lightly beaten

1. Cut a small piece from the top of each tomato. Set tops aside and carefully scoop out the seeds and pulp. Discard seeds. Place pulp in a small strainer, sprinkle with salt, allow to drain, and chop.

2. Salt the insides of the tomato shells, invert them on paper towels, and allow to drain for ½ hour.

3. Heat ¼ cup olive oil in a large skillet and sauté the onions and garlic for 8 minutes. Add the sausage and sauté until the meat has lost its red color. Drain fat from skillet and stir in the chopped tomato pulp. Cook 5 minutes more.

4. In a small bowl, stir the oregano, basil, parsley, and cheese into the bread crumbs until evenly blended. Add the milk and soak 5 minutes. Squeeze out the bread crumbs and discard the liquid.

5. Add the bread crumbs to the meat and cook for 5 minutes, stirring. Remove from heat.

6. When the mixture has cooled slightly, stir in the egg yolks, using a fork.

7. Stuff the tomato shells with the sausage mixture, sprinkle with olive oil, and cover with tomato tops.

8. Carefully place the tomatoes, sides touching, in a small baking pan. Bake at 350° F for 45 minutes.

Sausage-stuffed zucchini   *(Serves 6)*

Quick and easy to make, this is good as an appetizer, a side dish, or a main dish!

6 medium zucchini
1½ slices white bread, with crusts removed

1 pound Italian hot or sweet sausage, uncased
¾ cups grated Romano cheese
salt and pepper

1. Preheat oven to 350° F.
2. Scrub the zucchini and boil in salted water to cover for 5 minutes. Drain and pat dry.
3. Split each zucchini in half lengthwise. Scoop out the pulp, leaving the shell strong enough to stuff. Place pulp in bowl and set both pulp and shells aside.
4. Brown the sausage meat lightly, crumbling with a fork as it cooks.
5. Add to the zucchini pulp and mix.
6. Crumble the bread and mix with the zucchini.
7. Add the cheese, and salt and pepper to taste.
8. Stuff the shells with the sausage mixture and arrange in a well-buttered baking dish. Bake for 30 minutes and serve.

MAIN DISHES

Baked bockwurst   *(Serves 6)*

2¼ pounds bockwurst
1½ cups water

3 tablespoons bacon fat, melted
3 small onions, sliced

1. Place the sausage in a roasting pan.
2. Pour the water and bacon fat over the sausage.
3. Bake at 350° F for ½ hour.
4. Add the onions. Prick the sausage in a few places.
5. Bake for ½ hour more.
6. Cut the sausage into 6 pieces and arrange on a serving platter. Cover with the onions.
Serve with boiled potatoes and red, green, or savoy cabbage.

Bigos (Polish stew)   *(Serves 6)*

This is a hunter's stew, one of the oldest and best-known Polish national dishes.

10 dried mushrooms
¾ cup water
2½ pounds sauerkraut, fresh or
   canned
2 medium apples
6 black peppercorns

6 large, ripe tomatoes, quartered,
   or 1 (20-ounce) can whole,
   peeled tomatoes
1 bay leaf
5 cups diced kielbasa
6 slices bacon, chopped

1. In a small saucepan, soak the mushrooms in the water for about 2 hours. Then bring to boil, cover, reduce heat, and simmer for ½ hour. Drain, reserving the cooking liquid, and slice.

2. Rinse the sauerkraut in cold water and squeeze it to remove excess moisture. Place in a kettle or Dutch oven.

3. Add the mushrooms and the cooking liquid.

4. Peel, core, and slice the apples, and add them to the pot.

5. Add the peppercorns, tomatoes, and bay leaf. Bring to a boil, cover, reduce heat, and simmer for 1 hour.

6. Add the sausages and bacon. Cover and simmer for 1¼ hours more. Serve with boiled potatoes tossed lightly with butter and caraway seeds.

NOTE: This dish improves with reheating—you may even want to wait a day before serving it.

Bollito misto   *(Serves 6)*

In Italian, a "mixed-boil."

1 beef tongue, about 2 pounds
2 medium onions, whole
2 large carrots, peeled and cut in thirds
2 large stalks celery, cut into 2-inch chunks
1 pound boneless pork shoulder or loin
1 pound beef round

6 Italian sweet sausages
1 teaspoon freshly ground black pepper
¼ teaspoon garlic powder
¼ cup chopped parsley
1 medium head cabbage, cut in wedges
4 large potatoes, peeled and cut in half

133

1. Place the tongue in a large, heavy pot or kettle with water to cover. Bring just to a boil over high heat. Drain, return pot to stove, and cover tongue with boiling water.
2. Add the onions, carrots, and celery to the kettle. Bring to a boil again, cover, lower heat, and simmer for 1 hour.
3. Add the pork and beef, cover, and simmer for 1 hour more. Skim fat from top.
4. Add the sausages, pepper, and garlic powder, cover, and cook for 30 minutes.
5. Add the parsley, cabbage, and potatoes, mix well, cover, and cook for 30 minutes or until the potatoes are done.
6. Remove the meats and vegetables and arrange on a serving platter.
7. Strain the broth into individual bowls and serve as a side dish. Served with a French-style mustard.

Bratwurst with currant sauce   *(Serves 4)*

We've developed this ourselves. It has a unique sweet-sour flavor. Although it's good as a main dish, you can also serve it as an hors d'oeuvre.

½ cup currants
2 cups chicken stock
3 tablespoons cornstarch
3 tablespoons cold water
3 tablespoons vinegar

1 tablespoon honey (or syrup)
salt to taste
2 tablespoons butter
8 to 12 bratwurst

1. Simmer the currants in the chicken stock for ½ hour or until soft.
2. Dissolve the cornstarch in the water and add to stock. Stir well and continue stirring until the sauce has thickened, adding more cornstarch in water if necessary.

3. Add the vinegar, honey, and salt.
4. Stir in the butter. Remove sauce from heat, but keep warm.
5. Fry the bratwurst until nicely browned and cooked through.
6. Arrange on a platter and cover with sauce. Serve with white or brown rice or plain boiled potatoes.

Bratwurst with smoked pork chops   *(Serves 4)*

You can also make this with regular pork chops or with country-style spareribs.

½ pound bacon, chopped
1 large onion, finely chopped
1 pound sauerkraut
1 medium potato, peeled and
   grated
4 juniper berries

1 tablespoon caraway seeds
1 bay leaf
2 tablespoons sugar
4 large smoked pork chops
4 bratwurst

1. Fry the bacon in a large saucepan until lightly browned. Add the onion and cook until well browned.
2. Add the sauerkraut and enough water to cover. Mix well.
3. Add the potato, juniper berries, caraway seeds, bay leaf, and sugar. Bring to a boil, cover, reduce heat, and simmer for 1 hour.
4. Add the chops and bratwurst. Mix to cover with sauerkraut. Cook for 40 minutes more over medium-low heat.
5. Heap the sauerkraut in the center of a serving dish and alternate chops and bratwurst around it. Serve with potato dumplings or bread.

135

Cassoulet *(Serves 10)*

5 cups flageolets or small white beans
2 pounds pork loin
1½ pounds lean lamb
¼ pound salt pork
½ pound pork butt, cut into 1-inch cubes
1 bay leaf, broken in half
1 tablespoon minced parsley
1 teaspoon thyme
6 black peppercorns
1 clove garlic, whole
2 medium onions, each studded with 5 whole cloves
2 carrots, peeled and cut in half crosswise
2½ teaspoons salt
2 onions, chopped
2 cloves garlic, minced
1 cup tomato puree
1 cup beef bouillon
1 pound French garlic sausage
1 cup fresh bread crumbs

1. Place the beans in a heavy, deep, enamel or stainless steel kettle. Cover with water and soak overnight at room temperature.

2. Bone the pork loin, reserving the bones. Trim fat from meat and reserve. Cut the meat into 1-inch cubes. Repeat with the lamb.

3. Blanch the salt pork in water to cover. Drain and dice.

4. Add the diced salt pork and pork butt to the soaked beans.

5. Make a bouquet garni by tying the bay leaf, parsley, thyme, peppercorns, and garlic clove in a small piece of cheesecloth. Add to the kettle. Add the clove-studded onions, carrots, and salt.

6. Bring to a boil over high heat. Cover, lower heat, and simmer gently for 1½ hours. Remove bouquet garni, carrots, and onions, and discard.

7. Meanwhile, in a large, heavy skillet, render some of the fat trimmed from the pork, and brown the cubed pork, lamb, and bones very well.

8. Add the onions, garlic, tomato puree, and ½ cup of beef bouillon to the skillet and simmer, covered, for 1¼ hours. Remove bones and discard.

9. Add the skillet ingredients to the kettle and stir in the remaining ½ cup bouillon.

10. Prick the sausages and place in a skillet with water to cover. Simmer, covered, for 1 hour, drain and slice.

11. In another large, heavy kettle, alternate layers of the meat/bean mixture with the sliced sausages. Finish with sausages, top with bread crumbs, and bring to a boil on top of the stove.

12. Bake at 375° F for 1 hour. Serve hot.

Chorizos and white beans *(Serves 6)*

This is a traditional Spanish dish, served for lunch or a light supper.

2 cups dried white beans
1 medium onion, halved
4 large cloves garlic, whole
1 bay leaf
¼ cup olive oil

1½ tablespoons flour
3 pounds chorizo
2 teaspoons salt
½ teaspoon freshly ground black
    pepper

1. Place the beans in a large kettle. Add water until about 2½ inches above the beans. Add 1 onion half, the garlic, and bay leaf. Cover and bring to a boil, reduce heat, and sim-

mer, uncovered, until the beans are tender, 2 to 2½ hours. When the beans are almost done, remove the onion, garlic, and bay leaf, and discard.

2. Meanwhile, finely chop the other onion half, and sauté in the olive oil until tender. Remove from the pan, reserving the oil. Force the onion through a sieve, or puree in a blender.

3. In the reserved oil, brown the flour. Add a few tablespoons of cooking liquid from the beans, mix well and add to beans.

4. Add the onion puree to the beans and mix well.

5. Add the chorizo and boil gently for 15 minutes.

6. Drain the beans. Slice the chorizo.

7. To serve, put beans in individual bowls and arrange chorizo on top.

Choucroute garnie   (Serves 6)

This is an Alsatian specialty. Sometimes smoked pork chops are added.

2½ pounds sauerkraut, preferably fresh
1½ cups thinly sliced onion
1 clove garlic, crushed
2 tablespoons bacon fat
⅓ cup gin
½ teaspoon whole black peppercorns

2 medium-sized McIntosh apples
2 cups dry white wine
¼ cup kirsch
12 frankfurters, or a combination of frankfurters and knackwurst
1 tablespoon butter
1 teaspoon caraway seeds

1. Soak sauerkraut in cold water for 10 minutes, rinse, and squeeze as dry as possible.

2. Melt the bacon fat in a large, heavy saucepan and sauté the onions and garlic over medium-high heat.

3. When the onions are soft, add the sauerkraut and mix well. Add the gin and peppercorns and simmer for 5 minutes, stirring often.

4. Peel, core, and chop the apples and add to the sauerkraut. Add the white wine and kirsch, stir, and simmer slowly, covered, for 1 hour.

5. In a heavy skillet, fry the frankfurters in the butter until evenly browned. Add to the pot with the sauerkraut and simmer for 20 minutes more.

6. Remove the frankfurters and toss the sauerkraut with the caraway seeds. Arrange on a heated platter and serve with boiled potatoes, mustard, and rye bread.

Cornish hens with savoy cabbage *(Serves 4)*

You can also make this with ordinary cabbage.

1½ pounds lean Canadian bacon sliced ¼ inch thick
4 Cornish game hens
1 pound French garlic sausage
1 head savoy cabbage
4 carrots, quartered and cut in strips

4 stalks of celery, quartered
6 small white onions, whole
6 whole cloves
salt and pepper to taste
butter
¾ cup water

1. Preheat oven to 350° F.
2. Fry the bacon to a golden color, drain, and set aside.
3. Brown the hens in the bacon drippings and set aside.

139

4. Simmer the sausage in water to cover for about 5 minutes. Drain and cut into 8 pieces. Set aside.

5. Core the cabbage and place in a pot with water to cover. Add 2 more cups water. Boil for 7 minutes.

6. Remove the cabbage and peel off the leaves, one by one, dropping them in cold water as you go. Drain them all and pat dry.

7. Line the bottom of a shallow casserole with a layer of cabbage leaves. Arrange bacon slices on top of the cabbage, then the hens, breast side up.

8. Arrange carrots and celery around the hens.

9. Stick each onion with a clove and add to the other vegetables. Sprinkle with salt and pepper.

10. Cover with a second layer of cabbage.

11. Place the sausage pieces on top of the second layer, then cover with a final layer of cabbage leaves.

12. Dot with butter and sprinkle with more salt and pepper.

13. Pour in the water, cover the casserole, and bake for 1 hour or until the hens are done. Serve with the liquid.

Eggah with sausages   *(Serves 4 to 5)*

Eggah is a Tunisian dish with infinite variations. This is our favorite.

⅓ cup olive oil
½ pound new potatoes, peeled and sliced
¼ cup tomato paste
4 cloves garlic, cut in quarters
2 teaspoons caraway seeds
1½ teaspoons sweet paprika
¼ teaspoon cayenne

¼ teaspoon dried hot red pepper flakes
½ teaspoon freshly ground black pepper
⅓ cup water
8 Italian hot sausages
6 eggs, beaten
salt

1. Heat the oil over medium-high heat in a large, heavy skillet. Add the potatoes and sauté until lightly golden and crisp. Add the tomato paste and mix carefully to avoid crushing potatoes.
2. In a mortar, crush together the garlic, caraway seeds, paprika, cayenne, hot pepper flakes, and black pepper. Add to the potatoes and stir to blend well. Pour in the water, cover, and cook over the lowest heat possible for 15 minutes.
3. Meanwhile, put the sausages in another heavy skillet with water to cover. Bring to a boil, cover, and simmer for 10 minutes over medium heat. Drain, return skillet to burner, and brown the sausages evenly in their own fat. Drain.
4. Add the sausages to the potatoes, cover, and cook for 10 minutes over medium heat.
5. Slowly pour the beaten eggs into the skillet. Cook, stirring, until set but still soft.
6. Salt the eggah to taste and serve hot, right from the pan, with pita bread and a salad.

141

Enchiladas stuffed with chorizo *(Serves 6)*

2 pounds chorizo, uncased
1 large potato, finely chopped
2 medium Spanish onions, finely
  chopped
1 large green pepper, diced
vegetable shortening

12 tortillas, fresh or frozen
½ pound jack cheese, grated
 1 14-ounce can enchilada sauce,
    mild or hot (or your own spicy
    tomato sauce)

1. Cover the bottom of a skillet with water and add the sausage meat. Sauté and mash with a fork or spoon until crumbled into small pieces. Drain off excess fat.
2. Add the potato, half the onion, and the green pepper, and sauté for 5 minutes or until the vegetables are tender and the chorizo is well browned. Set aside.
3. Preheat oven to 350° F.
4. Melt shortening in a skillet to a depth of ¼ inch. Add a tortilla and cook for about 20 seconds to soften. Drain. Or soften by placing the tortilla directly on the burner over low heat, turning once.
5. Place a heaping tablespoon of the chorizo mixture in the center of the tortilla. Top with some chopped onion and grated cheese. Roll as for a crêpe and lay seam-side down in a casserole.
6. Cover with enchilada sauce and sprinkle with any remaining chorizo mixture, onion, and cheese.
7. Bake for 15 to 20 minutes. Serve with steamed or fried tortillas.

Garlic sausage in brioche   (Serves 4)

You can make this with frankfurters, knackwurst, or even bologna.

½ cup light cream
½ cup butter, softened
⅓ cup sugar
½ teaspoon salt
 1 package dry yeast
¼ cup warm water
 1 egg yolk

3 eggs, beaten
3¼ cups flour
 1 large (15- to 18-inch) French garlic
   sausage
Dijon mustard
 1 egg, beaten

1. Scald the cream and cool to lukewarm.
2. Cream together the butter, sugar, and salt.
3. Pour water in a large bowl. Sprinkle yeast in, let stand for a few minutes, then stir to dissolve.
4. Stir in lukewarm cream and the butter mixture.
5. Beat in the egg yolk and eggs.
6. Add the flour a little at a time, until thoroughly blended.
7. Cover and let rise 2 hours or until doubled in bulk.
8. Stir down with a wooden spoon, and beat thoroughly. Cover tightly and refrigerate for 24 hours.
9. The next day, poach the sausage in water for 40 minutes. (If you're using a precooked sausage, just heat it.) Remove from water, pat dry, and cool.
10. Preheat oven to 375° F.
11. Remove dough from refrigerator, stir down, and turn onto a floured board. Roll

143

½ inch thick, long and wide enough to enclose sausage.

12. Spread with a thin layer of Dijon mustard.

13. Place the sausage in the center and tuck in the sides of the dough. Bring the ends together, seal with water, and press closed. The dough should fit loosely.

14. Turn the encased sausage over and place on a greased cookie sheet. Brush with beaten egg to glaze.

15. Bake 30 to 40 minutes, or until done. Serve with hot potato salad or a spinach salad.

Gratin de saucisson   *(Serves 4)*

¼ cup butter
¾ cup onions, cut in half and sliced
  paper thin
¼ teaspoon olive oil
½ pound new potatoes, peeled and
  sliced
 1 cup sliced kielbasa, or other
  spicy sausage

1½ cups heavy cream
 ½ teaspoon salt
 ¼ teaspoon white pepper
  3 eggs
 ½ cup grated Swiss cheese
  1 tablespoon bread crumbs

1. Melt 3 tablespoons butter in a skillet, add the onions, and sauté slowly until tender. Do not let the onions brown.
2. Fill a medium-sized saucepan with salted water and bring to a boil. Add the olive oil, drop in potato slices, and boil for 7 minutes. Drain.
3. Preheat oven to 350° F.
4. Butter an 8-inch gratin or baking dish. Make an even layer in the bottom, using half the sliced potatoes topped by half the onion. Spread the sausage slices evenly and cover with another layer of onion, followed by the remaining potatoes.
5. In a medium-sized bowl, mix the cream, salt, and pepper with the eggs, and beat well. Pour over the ingredients in the dish, tipping the dish slightly to make sure the liquid reaches the bottom.
6. Spread the cheese evenly over the top and sprinkle with the bread crumbs.
7. Melt the last tablespoon of butter and drizzle over the cheese and bread crumbs. Bake for 35 minutes. Raise heat to broil for the last 5 minutes of cooking time.

Guatemalan sausage with rice and refried beans   (Serves 4)

Remember you need to plan for this one day ahead because the beans will need soaking time.

2 cups dried pinto beans
½ pound bacon
2 onions, finely chopped
1 green pepper, chopped
2 cloves garlic, minced
1 teaspoon salt

1½ teaspoons chili powder
½ teaspoon cayenne
2 Guatelmalan sausages (morango or longaniza)
2 cups cooked white or brown rice

1. Soak the beans overnight in 1½ quarts water in an enamel or stainless steel pot.
2. The next day, bring to a boil, cover, and simmer for 1½ to 2 hours or until the beans are tender.
3. Drain, reserving 1 cup of liquid (add water if necessary to make 1 cup). Set beans and liquid aside.
4. In a large, heavy skillet, fry the bacon until crisp. Drain and set aside.
5. Sauté the onion, green pepper, and garlic in the bacon fat until soft, but not browned.
6. Add the beans, bacon, salt, chili powder, and cayenne. Cook over medium heat, adding reserved bean liquid a little at a time. Stir and mash up the beans as they cook to get a mixture that is thick and almost creamy.
7. Meanwhile, boil the sausages in water to cover for 5 minutes. Drain the sausages and fry in their own fat until nicely browned and cooked through.
8. Serve the sausages with the refried beans and rice. Garnish with parsley.

Hot dogs and hominy *(Serves 4)*

Hominy is made of corn that has been hulled, dried, and degermed. Like the refried beans, the hominy must be soaked overnight.

1 cup dried hominy
1 pound hot dogs
1 pound fresh peas, shelled
½ cup melted butter

6 slices bacon, fried and crumbled
½ cup coarsely grated cheddar cheese

1. Soak the hominy overnight in 4 cups water in an enamel or stainless steel pot.
2. The next day, bring to a boil, cover, and simmer for 4 hours or until tender.
3. Preheat oven to 350° F.
4. Thoroughly butter a 3-quart casserole.
5. Brush the hot dogs with 2 or 3 tablespoons of the melted butter and score each 4 or 5 times with a sharp knife.
6. Fill the casserole with 3 wedge-shaped areas—1 of hot dogs, 1 of hominy, and 1 of peas.
7. Pour the remaining butter over the hominy and peas.
8. Sprinkle the bacon over the top.
9. Cover and bake for 20 minutes.
10. Uncover, sprinkle with the cheese, and bake, uncovered, for 5 minutes more or until the cheese melts.

Irish pork sausage with boxty (*Serves 6*)

3 tablespoons butter
12 Irish pork sausages
2 cups flour
4 teaspoons baking powder
3½ teaspoons salt

6 to 8 medium potatoes
1½ cups mashed potatoes
4 eggs, beaten
½ cup milk
8 tablespoons butter (approximately)

1. Melt the 3 tablespoons butter in a heavy skillet over high heat. Lower heat to medium-high and brown the sausages evenly. Set aside and keep warm.
2. Sift together the flour, baking powder, and salt. Set aside.
3. Grate enough potatoes to yield 2 cups. Wrap the grated potatoes in cheesecloth and squeeze to remove as much moisture as possible.
4. In a large bowl, combine the grated and mashed potatoes. Blend in the dry ingredients and the beaten eggs.
5. Add the milk a little at a time, to form a batter.
6. Melt 2 tablespoons butter in a heavy skillet. Drop the batter into the pan by tablespoonfuls and cook over medium heat, about 4 minutes on each side, until browned and crisp. Add butter to pan as needed. (Don't skimp on the butter here. The more buttery these are, the better.) Serve with the sausages.

Italian hot sausage with fennel   *(Serves 4)*

As a variation, substitute cauliflower flowerets and strips of green pepper for the fennel.

12 Italian hot sausages
 1 bunch fennel, cut into 4 pieces
 3 tablespoons olive oil
 3 onions, sliced in half rounds
 3 cloves garlic, minced
1½ teaspoons basil

2 teaspoons rosemary
1½ teaspoons fennel seeds, crushed
 1 teaspoon chopped parsley
 ¾ cup wine vinegar
 1 cup tomato paste

1. Place the sausages in a skillet with water to cover. Bring to a boil, simmer for 5 minutes, and drain.

2. In the same skillet, fry the sausages until nicely browned and cooked through. Remove and set aside to cool. Drain excess oil from skillet, but do not clean it.

3. Meanwhile, bring 1 quart of water to a boil and plunge in the fennel. Cook for 2 to 3 minutes. Drain and set aside.

4. Cut the cooled sausages in half lengthwise and set aside.

5. Heat the olive oil in the skillet in which the sausages were fried. Add the fennel and cook until lightly browned, then add the onions and cook until they are soft, but not browned.

6. Add the garlic, basil, rosemary, fennel seeds, parsley, and vinegar, and cook over low heat for 3 to 5 minutes, stirring constantly.

7. Mix the tomato paste with an equal amount of water and add to the skillet. Cover and simmer for 5 minutes.

8. Add the sliced sausages, cover, and cook over medium heat for 5 minutes more.

149

Italian hot sausage with kidney beans   *(Serves 6)*

You can make this with sweet sausages, too. If you do, add ¼ teaspoon pepper.

2 pounds Italian hot sausage
4 tablespoons olive oil
1 6-ounce can tomato paste
½ teaspoon salt

6 cups kidney beans, cooked and
    drained, with ¼ cup reserved
    cooking liquid
¼ cup red table wine

1. Prick the sausages and place in a skillet with water to cover. Bring to a boil, reduce heat, and simmer about 5 minutes. Drain.
2. In the same skillet, fry the sausages over medium heat until nicely browned and cooked through. Remove from skillet and keep warm.
3. Add the oil to the fat in the skillet.
4. Stir in the tomato paste, salt, and 1 tomato-paste can water. Cook for 10 minutes over low heat.
5. Add the kidney beans, bean liquid, and wine. Stir well.
6. Return the sausages to pan, cover, and simmer for 15 to 20 minutes.

Italian sausage omelet   *(Serves 4)*

1 large onion, cut in half and
    sliced
4 tablespoons butter
4 fresh tomatoes, chopped
1 pound fresh mushrooms,
    sliced

1 pound Italian sweet sausage, un-
    cased (or Helena Troy's sausages)
8 large eggs
½ cup milk
1½ tablespoons chopped parsley
    salt and pepper to taste

1. Sauté the onion in 2 tablespoons butter until soft, but not browned.
2. Add the tomatoes, mushrooms, and sausage meat and cook for 15 minutes, stirring occasionally to prevent sticking. Set aside and keep warm.
3. Beat together the eggs, milk, parsley, salt, and pepper.
4. Melt the remaining 2 tablespoons butter in a large skillet and heat until light brown.
5. Pour in the egg mixture, stirring rapidly until it begins to thicken. Stop stirring and cook for several minutes over medium heat, shaking the pan gently, until the eggs are done.
6. Remove from heat and pile the sausage mixture in the center. Fold the edges toward the center, forming a crêpelike tube. Place seam side down on a serving platter. Garnish with a few sprigs of Italian parsley and serve.

Italian sweet sausage hash   *(Serves 4)*

6 to 8 Italian sweet sausages
    4 tablespoons olive oil
    4 cloves garlic, minced
    1 onion, finely chopped
4 to 6 potatoes (2 to 3 cups), peeled and diced
    ½ pound mushrooms, sliced
    3 sweet red peppers, diced

2½ cups tomato sauce, homemade or canned
    1 tablespoon finely chopped Italian parsley
    1 tablespoon finely chopped fresh basil
salt and pepper to taste

1. Cut the sausages into bite-sized pieces.
2. Heat the oil in a heavy skillet. Add the sausage, garlic, and onion, and sauté over medium heat until the sausage is nicely browned.

3. Add the potatoes, mushrooms, and pepper and sauté for another 5 minutes, stirring frequently.

4. Add the tomato sauce, parsley, basil, and salt and pepper. Cover and cook over low heat for 20 to 30 minutes, or until the sausages are cooked through and the potatoes are done.

Italian sweet sausage with artichoke hearts   *(Serves 4)*

2 tablespoons butter
2 tablespoons olive oil
1 pound Italian sweet sausage, cut into ½-inch rounds
2 cloves garlic, minced
½ cup minced onion
1 tablespoon pine nuts
¼ pound fresh mushrooms, coarsely chopped

½ cup dry white wine
1 15-ounce can artichoke hearts, drained
½ cup minced parsley
1 10½-ounce can beef bouillon, un-diluted (or use your own beef stock)
½ cup grated Parmesan or Romano cheese
3 cups cooked white rice

1. Melt the butter in the olive oil in a large, heavy skillet. Add the sausages, garlic, onion, and pine nuts, and sauté lightly.

2. Meanwhile, simmer the mushrooms in the wine for 5 minutes. Drain, discarding the liquid.

3. Add the artichoke hearts, mushrooms, parsley, and ½ cup of the bouillon to the sausage skillet and simmer for 10 minutes over medium-low heat.

4. In a 2-quart casserole or soufflé dish, combine the contents of the skillet with the remaining bouillon, ¼ cup of the cheese, and the rice. Sprinkle the remaining cheese over the top and bake at 350° F for 25 minutes. Serve hot.

Kielbasa and potatoes   *(Serves 6)*

1 garlic clove, minced
1¾ cups minced onion
1 cup diced green pepper
½ cup bacon fat (approximately)
1 cup chopped ripe tomatoes

3 teaspoons sweet paprika
1½ pounds kielbasa, thinly sliced
2½ pounds new potatoes, peeled and sliced
1¼ cups water

1. Preheat oven to 425° F.
2. In a heavy skillet, sauté the garlic, onion, and green pepper in ¼ cup of the bacon fat for 5 minutes. Add the tomatoes and sauté 5 minutes more. Stir in paprika and set aside.
3. In a bowl, mix the kielbasa with the potatoes.
4. Grease a large, deep baking dish with bacon fat and build alternate layers of the tomato/onion mixture and the kielbasa/potato mixture.
5. Add the water and drizzle with bacon fat. Cover with foil and bake for 15 minutes. Reduce heat to 400° and bake for 25 minutes more, removing the foil for the last 10 minutes.
6. Brown lightly under broiler and serve hot with salad.

Kielbasa and red cabbage   *(Serves 4)*

This can also be made with bratwurst or bockwurst.

1 large head red cabbage
2 or 3 medium-large onions, sliced
2 tablespoons oil
3 tablespoons sugar
2½ tablespoons white vinegar

3 apples, sliced
salt and pepper to taste
1½ tablespoons caraway seeds
1½ pounds kielbasa

153

1. Shred the cabbage and set aside.
2. In a large kettle, brown the onions in the oil.
3. Add the sugar and cabbage and cook over medium heat, stirring occasionally.
4. When the cabbage is soft, add the vinegar and enough water to cover. Mix well.
5. Stir in the apples, salt, pepper, and caraway seeds. Cover and simmer slowly for 1 to 1½ hours. Taste and correct seasonings, if necessary.
6. Slice the sausage into 3-inch pieces and put on top of cabbage.
7. Cover and cook for another 15 to 20 minutes.
8. Serve with boiled new potatoes or parsley potatoes.

Kielbasa in red wine   *(Serves 4 to 6)*

3 cups red table wine
1 cup green onions, finely chopped
1 large (3-pound) kielbasa

1. Pour the wine into a heavy skillet and add the onions.
2. Add the kielbasa, uncut, and bring to a boil.
3. Lower heat and simmer for 35 minutes, or until the kielbasa is well glazed with the wine.
4. Remove the kielbasa and slice just before serving. Serve with pan juices and boiled potatoes, lightly buttered and tossed with caraway seeds.

Knackwurst omelet   *(Serves 4)*

2 medium onions, finely chopped
3 tablespoons butter
4 to 6 medium-sized boiled potatoes, cubed
4 knackwursts, cut into 1-inch rounds

6 eggs
¼ cup milk
4 tablespoons finely chopped parsley
salt and pepper to taste

1. In a large skillet, sauté the onions in butter until golden brown.
2. Add the potatoes and knackwurst and fry until nicely browned.
3. Beat the eggs and milk with a fork. Add the parsley, salt, and pepper and beat well.
4. Pour the egg mixture into skillet and cook, covered, over very low heat until the omelet is raised and fluffy and cooked through.
5. Cut into quarters and serve directly from skillet. Fresh cornbread or rye bread is a nice accompaniment.

155

Maltese sausage-rice bake   *(Serves 4)*

1½ cups raw rice
½ pound Italian sweet sausage
½ pound Italian hot sausage
¼ cup olive oil
¼ cup minced onion
2 cloves garlic, minced
¼ cup diced green pepper
2 cups beef broth
1½ cups tomato sauce

¼ cup tomato paste
2 large eggs, beaten
1 teaspoon salt
1 teaspoon freshly ground black pepper
1½ teaspoons sugar
¼ cup grated Parmesan or Romano cheese
½ cup pitted, sliced black olives

1. Soak the rice for 10 minutes in salted water to cover. Drain and place in a 2-quart casserole or a large soufflé dish.
2. Place the sausages in a large skillet and cover with water. Bring to a boil over high heat. Reduce heat to medium and simmer for 10 minutes. Drain.
3. Return skillet to burner and brown the sausages evenly in their own fat. Drain and, when cool enough to handle, slice into ½-inch rounds.
4. Heat the oil in another heavy skillet and sauté the onion, garlic, and green pepper for 5 minutes, stirring. Add the sausage slices and sauté 5 minutes more. Set aside.
5. Add the broth, tomato sauce, tomato paste, beaten eggs, salt, pepper, sugar, and cheese to the rice in the casserole. Stir well. Blend in the sausage mixture and mix again.
6. Bake at 350° F for 2 hours or until the rice is tender.
7. Arrange the sliced olives on the top and serve hot with more grated cheese, if desired.

Mediterranean sausage and chicken   *(Serves 6)*

As a variation, add anchovies to the sauce.

2 pounds Italian sausages, hot
  and sweet
1 chicken, cut in serving pieces
¼ cup olive oil
1½ cups chopped celery
4 onions, chopped
½ pound mushrooms, sliced

1 can sliced baby tomatoes
¾ cup pitted black olives
1 tablespoon capers
½ cup white wine
½ cup tomato paste
salt and pepper to taste

1. Cut the sausages in half lengthwise and fry until well browned. Drain and put in a heavy kettle.

2. Fry the chicken pieces in the olive oil until lightly browned on all sides. Drain, reserving the fat, and add to the sausages in the kettle.

3. Cook the celery in salted water to cover until softened, but still crisp. Drain, reserving the liquid, and set aside.

4. Cook the onions and mushrooms in chicken fat until softened, but not browned. Add the tomatoes, olives, capers, wine, and tomato paste, and simmer for 10 to 12 minutes.

5. Pour the skillet mixture over the chicken and sausages. Add salt and pepper, cover, and cook for 35 to 40 minutes or until the chicken is done. Add some of the reserved celery liquid, if necessary.

Midwest farmhouse sausage and apples   *(Serves 4 to 6)*

1½ pounds Midwest farmhouse
    sausage, thoroughly chilled
¼ cup plus 2 tablespoons water
6 apples, preferably McIntosh

1 cup sugar
¼ cup flour
1 teaspoon cinnamon

1. Slice the sausage into ½-inch rounds immediately before cooking.
2. In a large, heavy skillet, cook the sausage slices in the water until they are nicely browned and the water has more or less evaporated. Remove from the pan with a slotted spoon and keep warm. Reserve the drippings in the pan.
3. Core the apples, but do not peel them. Slice them into rings. Dredge the apple slices with a mixture of the sugar, flour, and cinnamon.
4. Reheat the sausage drippings and sauté the apple slices until they are lightly caramelized. Remove from the heat. On a heated serving platter, alternate the sausage slices and apple rings and serve.

Midwest farmhouse sausages in white wine   *(Serves 8)*

As a variation, use Italian sweet sausages or fennel sausages.

2 cups beef broth
1 cup white wine
4 carrots, grated
1 stalk celery, finely chopped

3 large tomatoes, cut in wedges
16 to 20 Midwest farmhouse sausage
    links, sliced

158

1. In a large pot, combine the broth, wine, carrots, celery, and tomato wedges. Bring to a boil, cover, reduce heat, and simmer for 15 to 20 minutes.

2. Meanwhile, sauté the sausages in their own fat until nicely browned and cooked through. Drain and discard fat.

3. Add the sausages to the broth and simmer, covered, for 20 minutes more.

4. Serve over brown rice, polenta, or cornbread.

Minnesota sausage pasties   *(Serves 4 to 6)*

These probably evolved from the English Cornish pasty.

Pastry:
1¼ cups whole wheat flour
1¼ cups white flour
1¾ teaspoons salt
 1 cup + 1 tablespoon lard
 1 cup ice water

Filling:
 1 pound basic bulk sausage, uncased
 3 baking potatoes, peeled and cubed
½ cup cooked peas
 1 medium onion, minced
 1 teaspoon salt
 1 teaspoon freshly ground black pepper
¼ teaspoon garlic powder

1. Combine the flours with the salt in a large bowl. Cut in the lard, using 2 knives or a pastry blender, until the mixture resembles a coarse meal.

2. Add the ice water a little at a time, tossing with a fork until the water is absorbed.

3. Form the dough into a ball and press firmly with the heel of your hand until the lard is evenly distributed through the dough. Knead 2 turns on a floured surface, form into a ball again, wrap in waxed paper, and refrigerate for ½ hour.

159

4. In a medium-sized bowl, combine the sausage meat with the potatoes, peas, onion, salt, pepper, and garlic powder.

5. Preheat oven to 375° F.

6. Divide the dough into 6 parts and roll each piece out on a floured surface to form a 10-inch circle.

7. Divide the filling into 6 parts and mound evenly on half of each circle.

8. Moisten the edges of the circles with cold water and fold over to enclose filling. Press the edges together firmly and crimp with a fork.

9. Prick the top of each pasty and place on an oiled baking sheet. Bake for 45 minutes.

Missouri pork sausage and mashed chestnuts *(Serves 4)*

1 pound chestnuts, shelled and skinned
milk
2 stalks celery, chopped
1 medium onion, chopped
½ teaspoon anise
2 tablespoons butter

salt and pepper
4 tablespoons light cream
1½ cups celery, finely chopped
1 pound Missouri pork sausage links
¾ pound mushrooms, sliced
1 clove garlic, minced

1. Place the chestnuts in boiling milk to cover. Add the celery, onion, and anise, and cook until the chestnuts and vegetables are very tender. Drain.

2. Mash with the butter and salt and pepper to taste. Add the cream and beat until fluffy. Set aside and keep warm.

3. Boil the sausage links in water to cover for about 5 minutes. Drain off water, then

sauté sausages until well browned and cooked through. Set aside, reserving drippings, and keep warm.

4. Sauté the mushrooms and garlic in the pan drippings until golden.

5. Stir the celery into the chestnuts and heap them in the center of a serving platter. Encircle with sausage links. Arrange sautéed mushrooms over the top. Garnish with parsley and serve.

Norwegian cheese and sausage   *(Serves 3 to 4)*

½ pound small white
   onions
3 tablespoons butter

1 large Norwegian sausage or
   kielbasa
¾ pound Jarlsberg or similar cheese

1. Peel the onions and boil in water to cover for 3 to 4 minutes. Drain.

2. Sauté the onions in butter over medium heat until lightly browned, being careful not to break them.

3. Place the sausage in a circle around the edge of a cast iron skillet large enough to hold it.

4. Slit the sausage deeply at 1-inch intervals. Be careful not to slice through completely.

5. Put a 1-inch-thick slice of cheese in each slit of the sausage.

6. Fry over medium heat until the sausage is cooked through and the cheese is somewhat melted.

7. Fill the center of the skillet with onions for the last few minutes of frying.

Peas Portuguese   *(Serves 4)*

Our friend, Eileen Denver, made this and changed one of us from a confirmed pea hater into a fan. This is a colorful dish, with bright green peas, red sausages, and yellow and white eggs.

3 tablespoons butter
¾ cup finely chopped onion
1 cup chicken stock (or bouillon)
5 cups fresh or frozen peas
5 tablespoons finely chopped parsley

5 tablespoons finely chopped coriander
1 teaspoon sugar
salt and freshly ground black pepper
½ to ¾ pound chorizo, cut into ½-inch rounds
4 eggs

1. Melt the butter in a heavy skillet. Add the onion and sauté over medium heat until golden.
2. Stir in the stock, peas, parsley, coriander, sugar, and salt and pepper to taste.
3. Arrange the sausage slices in a ring around the edge of the skillet.
4. Bring to a boil over high heat. Reduce heat and simmer, uncovered, for 5 minutes.
5. Break one of the eggs into a small, shallow dish or saucer and slide carefully into the pan on top of peas. Repeat with the rest of the eggs, making sure to keep them separate. Sprinkle eggs with salt and pepper.
6. Cover and cook over medium-low heat for 3 to 5 minutes, until the eggs are done.
7. Serve right from skillet with warm cornbread.

Ratatouille with sausages   *(Serves 6)*

This is our version of the French classic. It needs to sit overnight to allow the flavors to blend, so plan ahead.

2½ pounds eggplant, or 2 pounds eggplant and ½ pound peeled, diced zucchini
salt
½ to ¾ cup olive oil
3 to 4 Bermuda onions, sliced
2 large green peppers, cut into julienne strips
2 large cans Italian-style plum tomatoes

3 cloves garlic, minced
1½ teaspoons sugar
½ teaspoon freshly ground black pepper
¼ cup red wine vinegar
1 teaspoon Tabasco sauce
12 Italian sweet sausages
6 hard-boiled eggs, peeled and halved
¼ cup minced Italian parsley

1. Peel the eggplant and cut into small cubes. Spread on a double thickness of paper towels. Salt evenly and allow eggplant to drain. After ½ hour, rinse with cold water and pat dry with paper or cloth towels.
2. In a large, heavy skillet, heat ¼ cup olive oil over medium heat. Add the onions and green pepper and cook slowly until tender, but not browned, stirring often.
3. In a second skillet, heat another ¼ cup olive oil over medium heat. Sauté the eggplant in 2 batches for 15 minutes each, or until tender and golden. Drain.
4. Coarsely chop the tomatoes. Add more oil to the second skillet, if necessary, add the tomatoes, garlic, sugar, and pepper, cover, and simmer for 20 minutes, stirring often.

163

5. Combine the tomato and eggplant mixtures. Add the vinegar and Tabasco and simmer for 10 minutes or until the liquid is somewhat reduced and the mixture has thickened.

6. Transfer to a large, ovenproof bowl and refrigerate overnight.

7. Next day, place the sausages in a heavy skillet with water to cover. Bring to a boil over high heat. Cover, reduce heat, and simmer for 10 minutes.

8. Drain the sausages. Return skillet to burner and brown the sausages evenly in their own fat. Drain.

9. Preheat oven to 375° F.

10. Press the sausages and egg halves, yolk-side up, gently into the top of the ratatouille. Sprinkle with parsley, then with olive oil. Bake for 20 minutes.

Rice with sausages and green olives   (Serves 4)

You can also add red wine to this.

2 pounds Italian fennel sausage
2 large onions, peeled and chopped
2 cloves garlic, minced
2 large green peppers, diced
2 cups raw rice
3 teaspoons chili powder

pinch of cayenne
pinch of cumin
1 quart chicken stock
1 cup sliced, green, pimiento-stuffed olives

1. Place the sausages in a large, heavy skillet with water to cover. Bring to a boil over high heat. Lower heat to medium, cover, and simmer for 10 minutes. Drain, return to burner and brown the sausages evenly in their own fat. Drain, reserving fat. Slice the sausages and set aside.

2. In a large, heavy pot or kettle, sauté the onion, garlic, and green pepper in ⅓ cup of the reserved fat until tender, but not browned.

3. Add the rice and 2 tablespoons fat to the kettle and sauté, stirring constantly, until the rice is golden and translucent. Stir in the chili, cayenne, and cumin, and sauté for 2 minutes more.

4. Stir in stock and olives. Add sausage, cover, and simmer 40 minutes. Serve hot.

Sausage Agnes Riddle   (Serves 4 to 6)

Our mother developed this homage to Italian sausages long before either of us was born.

¼ cup olive oil
6 large onions, cut in half and and sliced thinly
2 6-ounce cans tomato paste
water
12 Italian hot sausages
12 Italian sesame rolls or hamburger buns

1. Heat the olive oil in a large, cast iron skillet. Add the onions and sauté gently until they are soft, but not browned.

2. Add the tomato paste and 2 cans of water and mix well. Keep simmering, uncovered, over very low heat.

3. In a second skillet, place the sausages in a single layer with water to cover. Bring to a boil, reduce heat, and simmer, covered, for 5 minutes.

4. Drain off water and, in the same skillet, brown the sausages evenly in their own fat.

5. Transfer the sausages to the onion sauce. Cover and cook for 30 to 40 minutes.

6. To serve, split each sausage in half and place it split-side down on the bottom half of a roll or bun. Spoon on onion sauce and top with the other half of the roll.

Sausage flautas   *(Serves 8)*

This main dish has its own sausage recipe.

2½ pounds lean pork
3½ teaspoons chili powder
  3 tablespoons red wine vinegar
1½ teaspoons cumin
1½ tablespoons oregano

1½ tablespoons minced garlic
  2 teaspoons salt
  3 tablespoons oil
36 6-inch tortillas
   corn oil

1. Cube the pork and grind coarsely.
2. Combine with the chili powder and vinegar until evenly blended. Add the cumin, oregano, garlic, and salt, and blend thoroughly, using your hands. Try to work the meat as loosely as possible. It should not pack down.
3. Melt the lard in a heavy skillet over medium-high heat. Fry the sausage mixture for about 10 minutes, stirring to keep the meat from browning unevenly and to avoid large clumps of meat from forming.
4. When there is no more pink showing in the meat, remove from heat.
5. Pour about an inch of corn oil into a second skillet and heat until very hot.
6. While the oil is heating, warm the tortillas on an ungreased skillet or griddle, and stack on a plate in a warm oven.
7. Use two tortillas to form each flauta. Overlap them by about 3 inches:

166

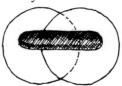

Form ⅓ to ½ cup of meat mixture into a sausage shape; center on tortillas as shown, and roll up. Secure well with 2 or 3 toothpicks per flauta.

8. Fry the flautas in the oil, a few at a time, for 2 minutes, or until golden in color. Drain and serve piping hot. These go well with rice.

Sausage croquettes *(Serves 8)*

6 large baking potatoes, peeled and quartered
3 tablespoons butter
¼ cup minced onion
¼ cup minced parsley
½ teaspoon garlic powder

2 egg yolks, lightly beaten
8 small sausages of your choice
bread crumbs
1 egg, beaten with 1 tablespoon milk
fat for deep frying
salt and pepper

1. Boil the potatoes in salted water until tender. Drain well and let the potatoes sit in the pot for ½ hour. Mash.
2. Melt the butter in a skillet and sauté the onion, parsley, and garlic powder until the onion is tender. Mash into the potatoes with the egg yolks. Chill.
3. Place the sausages in a heavy skillet with water to cover. Bring to a boil over high heat. Lower heat to medium, cover, and simmer for 10 minutes. Drain, return skillet to burner, and brown the sausages evenly in their own fat. Drain and cool.
4. Wrap each sausage in mashed potatoes. Roll in crumbs. Dip in beaten egg and roll in crumbs again. Chill for 2 hours.
5. Deep fry in hot fat until crisp and golden. Drain, add salt and pepper to taste, and serve.

167

Sausage marinara   (*Serves 4 to 6*)

¼ cup olive oil
1 large onion, chopped
2 or 3 cloves garlic, minced
2 teaspoons oregano
1 teaspoon basil
1 35-ounce can Italian-style
   plum tomatoes, chopped
1 6-ounce can tomato paste

1 teaspoon salt
1 teaspoon freshly ground black
   pepper
½ cup red wine
6 Italian hot sausages
6 Italian sweet sausages

1. Heat the olive oil in a heavy skillet and sauté the onion, garlic, oregano, and basil for about 15 minutes. Do not brown. Add the tomatoes, tomato paste, salt, pepper, and wine, and mix well. Cover and simmer over very low heat, the longer the better. Stir occasionally.

2. In a second skillet, bring the sausages to a boil in water to cover. Lower heat to medium, cover, and simmer for 10 minutes. Drain, return skillet to burner, and brown the sausages evenly in their own fat. Drain.

3. Add the sausages to the sauce and simmer, partly covered, for ½ hour. Serve with a pasta of your choice.

Sausage meat pie   *(Serves 4 to 6)*

This recipe was developed more than 100 years ago in the Deep South.

2 cups leftover roast beef, cut in ¾-inch cubes
2 tablespoons oil
2 cups onion bouillon
10 small pork sausages (we recommend Missouri pork or 2-inch slices of chaurice)
1 large onion, chopped
2 cloves garlic, minced
1 leek, sliced and separated into rings
¼ cup butter
¼ cup flour
salt and pepper to taste
1 cup parboiled potatoes, diced
¾ cup green beans, cut in 1-inch pieces
½ cup carrots, diced
pastry for a 9-inch, 2-crust pie
1 egg, beaten

1. Preheat oven to 425° F.
2. Heat the oil in a heavy skillet and brown the roast beef. Transfer to a large bowl and add the bouillon. Scrape the skillet drippings into the bowl and mix.
3. Place the sausages and about ½ cup water in the skillet. Simmer, covered, until most of the water evaporates. Uncover, increase heat, and brown the sausages in their own fat. Remove from pan and set aside.
4. Sauté the onion and garlic in the skillet until softened, adding more oil if needed. Add to beef and mix well.
5. Sauté the leek rings until transparent and set aside.
6. Drain the liquid from the beef, reserving 1¼ cups.

169

7. Melt the butter in a second skillet, add the flour, and cook until smooth and bubbling. Add the reserved liquid a little at a time, stirring constantly, until thick and smooth. Remove from heat and add salt and pepper.

8. Add the beef and onion, potatoes, green beans, and carrots. Mix together and set aside.

9. Roll out the pastry for bottom crust and line pie pan with it. Arrange 5 of the sausages in a star pattern on the crust. Spoon the beef and vegetable mixture evenly over the sausages. Top with the 5 remaining sausages, also arranged in a star shape.

10. Spread leek rings over all.

11. Cover with a top crust and seal. Make several slits or pierce all over with a fork to allow steam to escape while baking.

12. Brush beaten egg over the crust to glaze.

13. Bake for 15 minutes. Reduce heat to 350° F and continue to bake until the crust is golden brown.

Sausage quiche   (Serves 4 to 6)

Try this with different kinds of sausage—almost all are suitable.

pastry for a 9-inch, 1-crust pie
1 cup finely chopped cooked sausage (knackwurst, kielbasa, Irish pork, franks, or breakfast, or your own favorite)
½ cup thinly sliced onions
1 tablespoon chopped parsley

6 eggs
1½ cups heavy cream
1½ cups light cream
1 teaspoon salt
½ teaspoon freshly ground black pepper
¼ teaspoon nutmeg

1. Preheat oven to 400° F.
2. Line pie pan with the crust. Make sure it fits fairly loosely. Prick with a fork.
3. Line pie shell with aluminum foil and weight down with rice or beans to prevent air bubbles from forming (or place a second pie pan over the crust). Bake for 10 minutes. Remove from oven. Discard foil and rice or beans and lower oven temperature to 375° F.
4. Place the sausage, onion, and parsley in the shell.
5. Beat together the eggs, heavy cream, light cream, salt, pepper, and nutmeg, and pour into pie shell.
6. Bake for 30 minutes or until a knife inserted gently comes out clean.

Sausage ravioli   *(Yields about 4 dozen ravioli)*

As a variation, deep fry the ravioli and serve as canapés.

Filling:
  1 10-ounce package frozen chopped spinach
  ½ cup pine nuts
  2 tablespoons olive oil
  1 egg, lightly beaten
  1 cup ricotta cheese
  1 tablespoon grated Parmesan or Romano cheese
  2 pounds Italian sweet sausage, uncased

Pasta:
  4 cups all-purpose flour
  2 heaping teaspoons salt
  4 eggs
  1 tablespoon olive oil
  water

1. To prepare filling, cook spinach according to package directions, cool, and squeeze out excess moisture.

2. Heat the olive oil in a skillet and sauté the spinach and pine nuts for 5 minutes. Drain if necessary and grind or chop finely.

3. Blend the egg and ricotta cheese together with a wooden spoon. Add the Parmesan cheese and stir again.

4. In a large bowl, combine the sausage, spinach mixture, and cheese mixture. Blend well, using your hands. Set aside.

5. To prepare pasta, place the flour in a large bowl. Sprinkle the salt over the flour and make a well in the center. Drop in the eggs.

6. Beat the eggs into the flour with a wooden spoon. Add the olive oil and continue beating until well blended. Add water as needed to form a stiff dough.

7. Turn dough onto a floured board and knead for 10 minutes or until it is smooth, shiny, and elastic. Cover and set aside for 15 minutes.

8. Divide the dough into 2 equal parts. On a floured board, flatten 1 part slightly to form an oblong. Dust with flour. Roll out into a paper-thin oblong, being careful to flour the dough if it sticks.

9. Cover the rolled-out pasta with a damp cloth to keep it from drying out while you roll out the other dough in the same manner. Try to make it as close in size to the first piece as you can.

10. Place a small mound of filling every 2 inches in vertical and horizontal rows on one sheet of pasta. Dip a pastry brush or your finger in water and draw lines between the mounds, marking out squares. Keep the lines as even as possible. Carefully place the second sheet of pasta over the one with the mounded filling, pressing down carefully, but firmly, on the moistened lines. Using a pastry wheel or a sharp knife, cut along the lines. As the individual ravioli are cut, set aside on waxed paper.

11. Bring 6 quarts of salted water to a boil in a large pot. Carefully drop in the ravioli,

stirring gently and often to keep them from sticking. Test for doneness after 10 minutes. Drain and serve with your favorite tomato sauce.

Sausage ring with mashed limas   *(Serves 6)*

As a variation, substitute mashed sweet or white potatoes or turnips for the limas.

½ cup cornflake crumbs
1½ pounds pork sausage, uncased (we recommend Missouri pork or Midwest farmhouse)
1½ cups French bread crumbs
6 tablespoons minced onion
1½ teaspoons Dijon mustard

6 tablespoons chopped parsley
2 eggs, beaten with 1 tablespoon water
2½ cups fresh or frozen lima beans
⅔ cup cream
2 tablespoons butter
salt and pepper to taste

1. Preheat oven to 350° F.
2. Grease an 8-inch ring mold and press cornflake crumbs into the bottom.
3. Combine the sausage, French bread crumbs, onion, mustard, 5 tablespoons parsley, and the eggs.
4. Spoon and press sausage mixture into the mold. Bake for 35 to 40 minutes, draining off the fat after 15 minutes.
5. Prepare the limas about 15 minutes before mold is done. Cook at a rolling boil in 2 cups of water until very tender. Drain and mash or rice. Heat together the cream and butter and beat into the mashed beans. Add salt and pepper.
6. When the mold is done, remove from oven and run a knife around the inside and outside edges. Place a platter over the top and invert quickly. Let stand 1 minute. Tap

173

bottom of mold all over with a knife, then lift off mold. Use twisted paper towels to absorb any excess fat that runs off.

7. Heap mashed limas in the center of the ring. Garnish with a lump of butter and the remaining parsley and serve.

Sausages and apples   *(Serves 6)*

This is a lesser-known, but decidedly delicious, soul food dish.

1½ pounds pork sausage (we recommend Pennsylvania Dutch or Missouri pork)	8 large Rome Beauty apples brown sugar
½ pound bacon, diced	1 teaspoon cinnamon 1 teaspoon nutmeg

1. Fry the sausage until nicely browned and cooked through. Set aside and keep warm.
2. In another skillet, fry the bacon until browned, but not crisp.
3. Core the apples, but do not peel them. Slice and add to the bacon. Sweeten to taste with brown sugar.
4. Stir in the cinnamon and nutmeg.
5. Cover and simmer for about 15 minutes.
6. Uncover and brown the apples, turning them constantly, for about 10 minutes.
7. Heap the apples and bacon in the center of a serving platter. Surround with the sausages and serve.

Sausage-stuffed apples   *(Serves 4)*

4 large baking apples
1 cup sausage meat, uncased (we
  recommend bratwurst or
  knackwurst)

salt
cinnamon sugar

1. Preheat oven to 350° F.
2. Cut a slice off the top of each apple. Scoop out cores and flesh, leaving a shell strong enough to fill.
3. Cut flesh from cores and chop.
4. Combine the chopped apple with sausage meat.
5. Sprinkle the apple shells with salt and cinammon sugar.
6. Fill each shell with the sausage-apple mixture.
7. Place in a baking dish with a small amount of water in the bottom. Bake until just tender. Serve with rice, boiled potatoes, or buttered egg noodles.

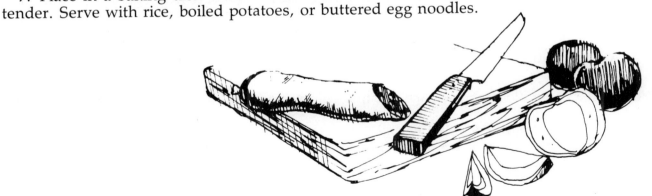

Sausage with rabbit   *(Serves 4)*

If you hunt, or if your butcher carries game meats, this is your dish.

1 large rabbit, skinned, cleaned,
and ready to cook
3 large onions, chopped
1 head red cabbage, quartered
4 large carrots, diced
1½ cups chicken, beef, or veal
stock (or bouillon)

salt and pepper to taste
1 cooked beet, grated, with juice
reserved
2 tablespoons cider vinegar
5 strips bacon
1¼ cups evaporated milk
¾ pound smoked sausages

1. In a large kettle, place the rabbit and ⅓ of the onions. Bring to a boil, cover, reduce heat, and simmer for 35 minutes. Remove the rabbit, strip the meat from the bones, and set aside.
2. Place the cabbage pieces in cold water to cover. Bring to a boil and cook for 5 minutes. Drain and chop coarsely.
3. Mix together the remaining onion, carrots, and stock. Add salt and pepper to taste and cook with cabbage until vegetables are tender.
4. Add the beet, beet juice, and vinegar.
5. Preheat oven to 350° F.
6. Line a casserole with the bacon strips. Fill with alternating layers of cabbage and rabbit meat.
7. Pour the evaporated milk over all.
8. Arrange the sausages on top.
9. Bake, uncovered, for 1½ hours.

Skewered knackwurst   *(Serves 8)*

8 knackwurst, each cut into 4 pieces
1 cup prepared French dressing
1 pound Canadian bacon, cut into small, thick chunks

24 to 30 pickled onions
24 to 30 tomato wedges
24 to 30 chunks of green pepper

1. Marinate the knackwurst in French dressing for 2 hours or more.
2. Skewer the knackwurst alternately with the remaining ingredients.
3. Barbecue or broil, turning often and brushing knackwurst with dressing, until done.

Sweet and sour bratwurst   *(Serves 4)*

As a variation, substitute 1½ tablespoons unsweetened pineapple juice for the vinegar, and add 1 cup pineapple chunks at the same time. Heat for 2 minutes longer.

8 bratwurst
½ teaspoon ground allspice
2 cups water
2 tablespoons butter (do not use margarine)

3 tablespoons flour
1 tablespoon granulated sugar
1 teaspoon brown sugar
½ teaspoon salt
1 tablespoon cider vinegar

1. Put the bratwurst and allspice in a medium-sized saucepan and add the water. Bring to a boil over high heat. Reduce heat and simmer gently for 20 minutes.
2. Remove the sausages and keep warm. Skim fat from pan and discard; reserve liquid.

177

3. Melt the butter over medium heat in a large, heavy skillet. Using a whisk, stir in the flour, a little at a time, to make a smooth roux. Cook, stirring constantly, for 3 minutes.

4. Add 1½ cups of the cooking liquid, ¼ cup at a time, stirring constantly with the whisk. Continue stirring and slowly bring to a boil.

5. When the sauce becomes thick and creamy, reduce heat to low. Add the sugars and salt and simmer for 2 minutes.

6. Slice the bratwurst thinly. Add to skillet and simmer for 2 minutes more. Add the vinegar immediately before serving.

Toad in the hole   *(Serves 6)*

This American favorite is actually of British origin.

6 tablespoons oil	½ teaspoon salt
12 links pork sausage (we recommend Midwest farmhouse or Pennsylvania Dutch)	1 cup milk
	1 cup light cream
1½ cups flour	2 large eggs, beaten
½ teaspoon baking powder	½ teaspoon nutmeg
	½ teaspoon mace

1. Preheat oven to 350° F. Heat 2 tablespoons oil in a skillet.

2. Cut each sausage link in half crosswise and sauté in oil until nicely browned. Remove, reserving drippings, and set aside.

3. Mix together the flour, baking powder, and salt. Stir in the milk, cream, eggs, and remaining oil. Add the nutmeg and mace and mix well. The batter should be smooth.

4. Pour about 4 tablespoons of the pan drippings into an 8-by-12-inch baking pan.

5. Pour in the batter.
6. Arrange the sausage pieces on top.
7. Bake for ½ hour or until the pastry puffs up and turns golden brown.
8. Serve immediately with crabapple or currant jelly or cranberry sauce as accompaniments.

Turkey and chaurice casserole   (Serves 6 to 8)

A soul food dish that's great for the day after Thanksgiving. If you don't have turkey, try it with chicken.

5 strips bacon
2 large onions, chopped
2 cloves garlic, minced
1 large green pepper, chopped
1½ pounds chaurice, uncased
4 cups turkey or chicken stock
4 cups light and dark turkey
   meat, cooked

2 cups raw white or brown rice
pinch of saffron
½ teaspoon onion powder
½ teaspoon cayenne
1 cup fresh green peas
salt and pepper to taste

1. In a large kettle or Dutch oven, fry the bacon until crisp. Drain and set aside. Pour off all but about 3 tablespoons of the drippings.
2. Brown the onions, garlic, green pepper, and sausage in the bacon dripings.
3. Stir in the stock, turkey meat, rice, spices, and peas. Add salt and pepper.
4. Crumble the bacon and sprinkle over top.
5. Simmer, uncovered, until the rice is done.

Veal cutlet with chorizo   *(Serves 4)*

It's hard to believe that something this good can be ready to serve in less than 1 hour.

1½ cups chicken broth
1½ cups beef broth
1 Bermuda onion, quartered
2 large green peppers, diced
4 cloves garlic, minced
½ teaspoon cayenne
1 tablespoon oregano

pinch of saffron
2 pounds thickly cut veal cutlets
flour
½ pound chorizo
salt and pepper to taste

1. In a large pot, place the broths, onion, green pepper, garlic, cayenne, oregano, and saffron. Bring to a boil, reduce heat, cover, and simmer for 15 minutes.

2. Dredge the cutlets with flour. Add the cutlets, chorizo, and salt and pepper to the broth.

3. Cover and cook for 15 minutes more, or until the veal and sausages are cooked through. Serve over boiled rice.

Vegetables and sausage parmesan   *(Serves 6)*

We developed this as a change from eggplant parmigiana.

3 tablespoons oil
1 medium eggplant, peeled and cut into strips
3 small zucchini, cut into strips
1 large green pepper, chopped
3 medium onions, sliced
1½ pounds Italian sausages, hot and sweet

1½ pounds Mozzarella cheese, sliced
3 cups tomato sauce, homemade or canned
salt and pepper to taste
1 teaspoon oregano
¼ cup Parmesan cheese, grated

1. Preheat oven to 350° F.
2. Heat the oil and add the vegetables. Sauté over medium heat until tender.
3. Sauté the sausages in a second skillet until well browned. Drain and slice each in half crosswise.
4. In a greased baking dish, alternate layers of vegetables, sausages, Mozzarella cheese, and sauce, sprinkling each layer with salt, pepper, and oregano.
5. Finish with a layer of sauce and sprinkle with Parmesan cheese.
6. Bake for 30 minutes, or until heated through.

Vietnamese sausage fried rice   *(Serves 4)*

8 dried Chinese mushrooms,
   either black or tree-ear type
vegetable oil
2 Chinese sausages, cut into
   ½-inch rounds (*see note below*)
1 medium onion, cut in half and
   sliced paper thin
4 cups cooked long-grain white
   rice
1 tablespoon oyster sauce
¼ cup soy sauce

½ teaspoon sesame oil
½ pound baby shrimp, shelled,
   cleaned, and coarsely chopped
1 cup crab meat, picked over to remove all shell and cartilage
3 eggs, beaten with 1 tablespoon
   water
¼ cup thinly sliced scallions
½ cup cooked peas
2 tablespoons minced chives

1. Soak the dried mushrooms in hot water to cover; drain when soft. Trim and cut into thin strips.

2. Heat 2 tablespoons oil over medium heat in a medium-sized skillet. Fry the sausage slices until crisp, about 3 minutes. Drain.

3. Heat ⅓ cup oil over medium-high heat in a large, heavy skillet or wok. Sauté the onions for 2 minutes, stirring to keep from burning or browning. Add the mushrooms and rice and sauté quickly, stirring. Stir in the oyster sauce, soy sauce, and sesame oil. Continue to sauté, stirring, until the rice is hot, about 2 minutes more. Remove the mixture from the pan and keep warm.

4. Add 2 tablespoons oil to the skillet or wok and sauté the shrimp and crabmeat, stirring constantly, for 5 minutes. Return the rice to the skillet and add the sausages. Mix together until evenly blended.

5. Add the eggs, a little at a time, stirring the entire mixture well with each addition. Stir in the scallions and peas.

6. Transfer to a large, heated platter, sprinkle with chives, and serve with additional soy sauce, if desired.

NOTE: This is the only place where we are giving you a recipe for a dish without providing the basic sausage recipe. Chinese pork sausages are made under such exacting conditions, including months of curing and drying, that it is not practical to make them yourself. They may, however, be purchased at specialty stores and Chinese groceries. They are delicious, and we wanted to give you a chance to use them. They also make a good appetizer when steamed and served with soy sauce.

DESSERTS

Bavarian sausage cake   *(Yields 1 tube cake)*

One of the few sausage desserts we've encountered. We were a little skeptical until we tried it.

Cake:

- 1 pound pork sausage, uncased (we recommend basic bulk sausage)
- 1¼ cups white raisins
- 2 cups water
- 1¾ cups firmly packed brown sugar
- 1 cup molasses
- ½ teaspoon cloves
- 2 teaspoons nutmeg
- ½ teaspoon allspice
- 1 teaspoon grated orange peel
- 4 cups white flour
- 1 teaspoon baking powder
- 1¼ cups shelled walnuts, coarsely chopped.

Icing:

- 4 ounces cream cheese
- 2 tablespoons heavy cream
- 1 cup confectioners' sugar, sifted
- 2 teaspoons grated orange peel

1. Preheat oven to 300° F.
2. Place the sausage meat and raisins in a bowl.
3. Bring the water to a boil and pour over the sausage and raisins. Cover and let steep for about 10 minutes.
4. Remove the cover, add the brown sugar, and stir until well blended.
5. Add the molasses and spices and blend well.
6. Sift together the flour and baking powder and add to the sausage mixture a little at a time, blending well after each addition. The batter should be stiff; add more flour if it isn't.
7. Stir in the walnuts.
8. Spoon the batter into an ungreased tube pan.
9. Bake for 1 to 1½ hours or until done. Remove from oven and let cool upside down on a rack. Remove from pan.
10. When the cake has cooled, prepare the icing. Work together the cream cheese and cream until softened and fluffy. Gradually add the confectioners' sugar, blending well after each addition. Add the orange peel and mix well. Ice the cake and serve.

Dessert sausage   *(Makes 4 to 6 sausages)*

This is a delicious fruit-and-nut sausage we concocted for Mary Jane's sons, John and Matthew; it will break any child of the junk-food habit. You can vary the nuts used to suit your preference.

1 cup shelled pecans
1 cup shelled almonds
1 cup pitted dates
1 cup chopped figs
1 cup chopped candied pineapple
½ cup golden raisins
½ cup currants
½ cup candied cherries
2 tablespoons minced crystallized ginger

1 teaspoon grated orange (or tangerine) rind
½ teaspoon cinnamon
¼ teaspoon nutmeg
½ teaspoon salt
2 teaspoons brandy (optional)
1 tablespoon honey
1 cup shredded coconut
1 cup chopped pistachio nuts

1. In a large bowl, blend together the pecans, almonds, dates, figs, pineapple, raisins, currants, and cherries. Grind coarsely.

2. Add the ginger, orange or tangerine rind, cinnamon, nutmeg, and salt, and mix with your hands until well blended. Add honey. Moisten with brandy if desired.

3. Divide the mixture in half and form 2 or 3 sausages from each half, adding more honey if necessary to bind ingredients. Make sure honey is evenly distributed through mixture. Roll half the sausages in shredded coconut and the others in chopped pistachio nuts. Wrap in plastic wrap, waxed paper, or colored cellophane. Slice to serve.

Recipe Index

189